CRIPPLED CHRISTIANITY

The Last Church Age Revelation

By DEMORY GREEN

Table of Contents

Introduction

Crippled Christianity.

Crippled Christianity?

Crippled Christianity!

What does it mean? Is it a statement of fact? A question? An accusation? Cause for alarm? For any professing Christian, even the possibility of Christianity being crippled ought to be of concern.

A statement like this would be cause for concern to the man who wrote much of the New Testament (the Apostle Paul), and to the One who commissioned him (Jesus). Let's have a talk about both.

Paul's standing as a powerful Christian is beyond question. He was dramatically commissioned by the Lord during a trip to persecute and violently snuff out the fledgling Christian movement. This trip included a life-changing, supernatural intervention like few experience (see Acts 9: 1-19).

That experience on the Damascus road set Paul on a new path that would take him on missionary trips across the Asian portion of the Roman Empire. He spent years establishing churches, receiving revelation, and writing the majority of the letters to churches that are now the New Testament books of the Bible.

Part of his race was to keep the accuracy of the gospel message. One thing Paul foresaw was heresy in the Christian Church that would try and pollute the gospel. Even when he was going to Jerusalem and ready to die, he warned *"that after my departure, savage wolves will come in among you, not sparing the flock. Also of your own selves shall men arise, speaking perverse things, to draw away disciples after them"* (Acts 20:29-30).

This was no surprise. Jesus, during his three-year ministry, also told His disciples to expect doctrinal challenges from within. And when the subject turned to the last days (our days), the expectation was for perilous conditions (see Matthew 24).

But Jesus expected the Christian Church should have a worldwide effect. He told his disciples, *"You will receive power when the Holy Spirit has come upon you; and you shall be My witnesses both in Jerusalem, and in all Judea and Samaria, and even to the remotest part of the earth"* (Acts 1:8).

And it wasn't to be any inconsequential, unnoticed thing:

> *Heal the sick, raise the dead, cleanse lepers, cast out demons. Freely you have received, freely give.*Matthew 10:8

> *And these signs will follow those who believe; In my Name they will cast out demons; they will speak with new tongues; they will take up serpents; and if they drink anything deadly, it will by no means hurt them; they will lay hands on the sick, and they will recover.*Mark 16: 17-18

For believers this was to be their new normal.

That is the race Paul spoke of, and not just his, but the Church's as a whole as well as every individual. Paul summarized the gospel thus in Ephesians 3: 8b-11:

> *That I should preach among the Gentiles* (the non-Jewish world) *the unsearchable riches of Christ, and to make all see what is the fellowship of the mystery, which from the beginning of the ages has been*

hidden in God who created all things
through Jesus Christ; to the intent that
now the manifold wisdom of God might
be made known to the principalities and
powers in the heavenly places. . .

Understanding and exercising this mystery is intended to impact not just people, but the unseen host of angelic and demonic beings! The Christian message is to be a kingdom disrupter!

So here's my point.

What's the state of Christianity's race, corporately and individually? How would the expert commentator in the upper box call the race?

Is the race being run effectively, or not?

Are the Church's efforts producing what the Lord intends?

In the last 200 years, the gospel message has expanded to reach nearly every part of the earth. There is probably nowhere in the world that it is not available via the Internet. Millions have been saved and are still being saved. But, as a normal thing, are the dead being raised at the hand of believers? The sick being healed? Signs, wonders and miracles happening? Messages delivered that cause thousands at a time to believe? The world population continues to expand; are we making any headway against that?

Is Christianity running its race well? Or is it running crippled?

We could go on at length here, but unless we indulge in making excuses, I believe it is clearly evident that, when measured against the commissioned purpose, Christianity as a whole is running crippled. Much of the Lord's harvest is still being lost.

And there is little time to get things fully functioning. While this is not a book on prophecy, there is a widespread awareness that present world events are strongly indicating Jesus' imminent return for the church. Analysis of God's timing indicates perspectives possibly as short as a year. Time is running out!

Something needs to change.

The effectiveness of how well any individual lives Christianity is always an individual evaluation and can only be evaluated by the Lord. Every man stands or falls to his own master (see Romans 14:4).

But if the results of the gospel message seem to be universally impaired, then the message needs a review.

It is time to see the 'fellowship of the mystery' that Paul desired so fervently all would understand and finally answer the question, "What is the gospel?"

This is a message to the Body of Christ.

Chapter One

Perspective

Personally charged by Jesus with the Great Commission to take the gospel to the ends of the earth, the first disciples needed an organized definition and defense to assemble the gospel into a recognizable picture to demonstrate.

The *definition* of the gospel was the first historical item of business. This was accomplished with eyewitness gospels, epistles, writings, and church councils who codified the accepted body of scripture and belief. With an enemy (Satan) intent on corrupting the message, people had to know what the real thing was. Without an accepted standard, the true message of salvation could be watered down, stolen and replaced with a believable imitation. This still holds true today.

The *defense* of the gospel is a continuing issue. Whether it's the historical process of assembling the written gospel accounts and epistles as our Bible, or the continuing verbal confrontations encountered in preaching the Word, the accuracy of the gospel message must be maintained and pressed against a pagan world steeped in demonic influence.

Meanwhile, the world's unseen master is intent on either destroying or corrupting the Christian message. That corrupting influence has been evident in several philosophical and religious camps throughout the centuries. These are always attempts to inject the gospel with denials of Christ's divinity or approvals for all manner of immoral behavior, along with half-truths that dilute the message and sap the demonstration of power.

When it comes to the daily *demonstration* of the gospel, there are two avenues commanded: to express the love of God to others and to do the same works that Jesus did with powerful signs, wonders, and miracles done by the Holy Spirit. Both demonstrations touch people where they live.

However, the tough part through Church history has been recognizing and agreeing on the *details* of the gospel—What exactly happened at Calvary? And in what way has it affected us? Why has it generated so much internal denominational friction over the years? Is it grace or mercy that embodies the Christian gospel? Which is God's true character?

Is there something overlooked that can settle these issues and give a single clear and rational picture? That is what we will accomplish in this book.

Foundations

As the completed end of the Jewish faith, Christianity's foundation is the Law and the Prophets of the Old Testament. We see this in Jesus' explicit qualification to His disciples:

> *Then He said to them, "These are the words which I spoke to you while I was still with you, that all things must be ful-filled which were written in the Law of Moses and the Prophets and the Psalms concerning Me."*   Luke 24:44

In this passage, it is immediately evident that this picture is in a legal frame. Israel's behavior was constrained by a body of law handed down directly from God. When the Israelites started cutting corners, they were called to account by God's prophets. Israel experienced some impressive miracles for their obedience, and some traumatic punishments for disobedience.

Thus the foundation of the Christian message is also seen, by default, as legal. This is why, understandably so, there was so much discussion in the Early Church about whether or not new believers had to keep all of the Law, or for a while, whether the message should even be taken outside the Jewish community.

Here is the first place we want to start checking the details. For illustrative purposes, if 'legal' were the coin that defines the framework for salvation, it could be said to have two sides—each with its own recognizable stamp—a heads and tails side. 'Legality' is the heads side, what I call the God side. 'Legalism' is tails, man's side. Just like using a coin for the toss to decide position on the field before a sports game, which side you look at will decide your position (or view) on Christianity.

Both views involve accountability to the Law (neither has any meaning apart from a body of law), but most people don't take time to distinguish between the two. (They both sound a little undesirable, don't they?) However, there is a very important reason to distinguish between them; while they are competing views of the same 'legal' field, both can be potential snares to a saving faith.

Legalism

Let's touch on legalism first, the snare that too easily entangles us. *Merriam-Webster's* dictionary defines it as "the strict, literal, or excessive conformity to a religious or moral code." Legalism says, "I did what the rules required, so I'm okay. I'm not responsible for anything outside of the Law!"

Have you known people like this? They are always looking for shortcuts that require minimum effort and responsibility. You can recognize these people because they believe the rules you are supposed to follow are a lot more involved than the rules they are supposed to follow!

Jesus, of course, had nothing positive to say about such people (especially the Pharisees and lawyers) who upheld a form of the law without obeying the true precepts of love and justice (see Luke 11:42-46).

There is nothing about legalism that would make someone outside of Christianity want to be a Christian. Legalism is the world's normal way of doing things.

Legality

Legality is the idea that, as long as justice is satisfied and the proper punishments have been handed out, nothing else is necessary. Legality is the picture commonly formed of God's side of the coin.

I make a point of saying it this way because legality involves an assumption about the character and motivation of God. The people of Israel fell prey to that snare. Psalm 103:7 goes to the heart of the matter: *"He made known His ways to Moses, His acts to the children of Israel."* Moses had a revelation of God's mercy and grace, but Israel never got past a shallow, surface view of His external actions. Without revelation of who God was, there was nothing but a law to constrain them sufficiently.

Legality ascribes to God an inflexible "righteousness" that demands punishment for every infraction. No crime goes unpunished—no matter how small or large—no exceptions. Someone has to be punished, and as long as someone is, whether the offender or another in his place, then God is satisfied.

One widely quoted verse asserting this view of God is Habakkuk 1:13, *"You are of purer eyes than to behold evil, and cannot look on wickedness."* Unfortunately, that is only half the verse. The whole verse in context shows that isn't God saying it of Himself, but the writer ascribing that to God and then complaining that God hasn't lowered the boom on someone else. The point is that an inaccurate assumption about God's character can leave people today just as separated from His mercy and grace as it did Israel.

The danger of both legality and legalism is that neither demands a change of heart, only a list of behaviors. And by settling for either view, the bottom-line desire of God's salvation is left unfulfilled. God wants our obedience to be from the heart. King David said of God, *"Behold, you desire truth in the inward parts, and in the hidden part You will make me know wisdom"* (Psalm 51:1).

Chapter Two

Two Audiences, Two Messages

———+>••<+———

A nother illustrative way to think of the legal foundation of the gospel message is as an organized sport. The body of the Law represents the rules of the game, the prophets' messages are the referees' calls, and legality and legalism are the out-of-bounds. And all of that foundation was for one purpose: to recognize and welcome the star player when He entered the field.

First Audience: The Jews

And so, for all the initial apostles, along with Paul, the first audience for the gospel was their own people, the Jews, those who were under the Law. Amid all the commotion that the gospel caused, the message to the Jews was simple: Jesus is the Redeemer, the Messiah, the Christ, the One written of in history;

the One all the Mosaic Law, the Prophets and the Psalms looked for and predicted. This was Jesus' witness of Himself as well. We see this in Matthew 5:17, when He said, *"Do not think that I came to destroy the Law or the Prophets. I did not come to destroy but to fulfill."*

Chapter 5 of the book of Acts records the furious resistance of religious leaders as Peter and the other apostles spread the message. At one point, the religious council plotted to kill them, but a respected teacher (Gamaliel), advised them to wait and see if the movement was of God or not. After beating the apostles and threatening them to speak no more in the name of Jesus, they let them go. But the persecution did not deter the apostles, *"and daily in the temple, and in every house, they did not cease teaching and preaching Jesus as the Christ"* (Acts 5:42).

Relating Paul's preaching after his supernatural commission from the Lord, Acts 9:22 summarizes: *"But Saul (Paul) increased all the more in strength, and confounded the Jews who dwelt in Damascus, proving that this Jesus is the Christ."*

As I mentioned before, the whole point of the Law and the Prophets boiled down to the one simple thing: recognizing the star player when he came on the field. Looking at the David versus Goliath confrontation as a type of Jesus' arrival to challenge the evil *and* religion of the day, we can see Jesus was our team's *only* player!

Still, as Jesus said, the Law had to be fulfilled.

Remember we made a point of talking about the two sides of the legal coin? When it came down to the day of recognizing and welcoming the Messiah, the religious hierarchy of scribes, Pharisees, and Sadducees made legalism their defense, and legality the sum-total of God's position (motivated by preserving the power they held over the people). Interestingly, the important conclusion that even the corrupted religious leaders of Jesus' day voiced is that justice demanded a settlement, even if it was through a substitute.

> *And one of them, Caiaphas, being high priest that year, said to them, "You know nothing at all, nor do you consider that it is expedient for us that one man should die for the people, and not that the whole nation should perish.*
>
> John 11:49-50

With the benefit of broader understanding, John continues,

> *Now this he did not say on his own*
> *authority; but being high priest that*
> *year he prophesied that Jesus would*
> *die **for the nation**.*   V. 51

To get an accurate view of the message to the first audience, let's look at two other scriptures, since nothing is true except by the testimony of two or three witnesses (*see* Deuteronomy 17:6, Hebrews 10:28).

The salvation message focuses on Christ at the cross. The crucifixion combines a judicial assumption with an emotional presentation of the vicious beatings and horrible physical torture. However, when that kind of picture is presented, emotion usually trumps reason, and the unseen supernatural component gets overlooked.

If Jesus came, as He said, to fulfill the Law and the Prophets, then the only way to clearly understand the whole picture of the gospel is to find out what the Law and the Prophets required. The brutality of the crucifixion is emotionally moving, but it was a necessity brought on by Israel's disobedience. Without negating or denying the ugly physical realities of the crucifixion, there are vital, but rarely-made, observations from 2 Samuel 7 and Psalm 89 that allow the mystery of the salvation message to be understood.

In both of these scriptures, God is speaking to King David regarding potential misdeeds of both David and his son, Solomon (as well as other descendants), and the punishments that would be exacted.

Let's look first at the key verses within 2 Samuel 7:

> *Now therefore, thus shall you say to **My servant David**, "Thus says the Lord of hosts: "I took you from the sheepfold, from following sheep, to be a ruler over My people, over Israel.... When your days are fulfilled and you rest with your fathers, I will set up **your seed after you,** who will come from your body, and I will establish his kingdom.... I will be his Father, and he shall be My son. **If he** [Solomon] **commits iniquity, I will chasten him with the rod of men and with the blows of the sons of men.***"*   *Vv. 8, 12, 14*

As a psalmist, David refers to this agreement he had with God again in Psalms 89:

> *I have made a covenant with My chosen, I have sworn to **My servant David**:...*
> *"If **his sons** forsake My law and do not*

*walk in My judgments, If **they** break My
statutes and do not keep My command-
ments, **Then I will punish their trans-
gression with the rod, and their
iniquity with stripes.*** Vv. 3, 30-32

First, we see here that the crucifixion—the
brutal beatings and torture Jesus endured—was
for Israel's sake. It was specifically for David, his
son Solomon, his family and, by responsibility of
the king to act for the people, national Israel. There
was a price Israel had to pay for breaking the Law
given through Moses, and it was Jesus who paid it.

This means the crucifixion *was not* a universal
punishment by God for man's sinfulness. This is
evident when considering the Law's place in the
historical timeline, and the point that Paul made
in Galatians 3:19 about the Law being an addition
made necessary by Israel's disobedience.

From Adam to Jesus' arrival was roughly 4000
years, yet the Law given to Israel via Moses on their
exodus from Egypt took place in the last 430 years
before Christ. It would be a total travesty of justice
to hold 4000 years of the family tree responsible for
a law that hadn't even been given yet. Thus punishments for breaking the Law were binding only on

Jewish Israel from the Egyptian exodus on, since that's who agreed to be bound by the Law.

The pronouncements concerning David in the second Samuel verses represent an addition to the Law, this again, relevant only to Jewish Israel. And more directly to Paul's point, if the entire Law was an addition, there was something in place already that covered everyone from Adam forward.

Let me repeat it because this thought is central to understanding the mystery of salvation in Christianity. The vicious beatings, torture, and crucifixion of Christ did not represent a universal punishment for sin! Those were related to Jewish Israel. It may be hard to grasp now, but will be understood by the time you finish reading this book.

By not recognizing this reality, religion (while trying to be rational) has included a couple of dangerous assumptions in the gospel message.

One is the assumption that salvation hinges on one substitutionary punishment for all the world's individual acts of sin. However, merging all sin under a universal punishment obscures the separation between salvation (the mystery) and the judgment scene we find in Revelation 20:11-13, where rewards or punishments are meted out for the things done on earth. (We can also see this in Jesus' parable of the talents in Matthew 25:1-30 where a landowner left one, five, and ten talents respectively to three servants to invest. There was a performance reward when he returned.)

John states the basis for salvation clearly in John 3:18: "*He who believes in him is not condemned; but he who does not believe is* **condemned already**, *because he has not believed in the name of the only begotten Son of God.*" From the beginning of Genesis (3:15), the point of salvation was to recognize the seed of the woman when He appeared. That's tough to do when the message isn't passed accurately between generations, and especially in a day when our culture denies even the existence of God.

When the real ground for salvation is obscured, even within religious circles, it is too easy to lapse into a 'legalism' frame of mind, which negates both heaven and rewards!

More foundationally, I think it assigns a certain underlying inflexible, cold, viciousness about God that repels rational people, and makes "God loves you" sound a little hollow. (Although this seems to appeal to some religious groups, both Christian and non-Christian. The Muslim view of God is built on it.) When salvation is perceived to hinge only on actions, it seems that approval inevitably comes down to whatever the accepted social standards of the day are—how you dress, how you wear your hair, what you eat, whether you smoke, and so on. I know one person who, because he grew up with a family member like that, wants nothing to do with Christianity.

A second errant conclusion of an all-inclusive punishment involves what has been labeled as replacement theology. Replacement theology basically asserts that God is done with the Jews, having replaced them with Christians in his salvation dealings. Without stopping here to include a lengthy refutation, we will simply point out that the prophecies concerning Israel in these last days (the final seven days of Daniel's seventy weeks) have yet to be fulfilled. Jewish Israel and the Christian Church are still two separate groups, each with its own place in God's continuing dealings.

We can extract the same idea of misunderstanding the target audience for the crucifixion in another set of scriptures as well: Isaiah 53:3-5 and 1 Peter 2:24.

First Peter 2:24 says, "*Who Himself*[Jesus] *bore our sins in His own body on the tree, that we, having died to sins, might live for righteousness—by whose stripes* **you were healed**." When Peter wrote this, he was quoting from Isaiah 53:

> *He is despised and rejected by men, a Man of sorrows and acquainted with grief. And we hid, as it were, our faces*

*from Him; He was despised, and we did not esteem Him. Surely He has borne our griefs and carried our sorrows; Yet we esteemed Him stricken, Smitten of God, and afflicted. But He was wounded for our transgressions, He was bruised for our iniquities; the chastisement for our peace was upon Him, **and by His stripes we are healed.***   Vv. 3-5

Before tying these two scriptures with the flow of our subject, some things should be pointed out regarding both Isaiah's and Peter's writing.

Isaiah, quoted by Peter, was writing to Jewish Israel, not to the world at large. Peter was writing to Jewish believers. As we noted earlier, the beatings were the punishments for David, his son Solomon, and his bloodline for not keeping the Law—for Jewish Israel, not as a universal punishment for mankind's sinful acts.

For this passage, it also helps to know that Peter wrote this at a time when the pagan religions of the day asserted that Jesus didn't really come in the flesh, only in some immaterial, visible form. In 1 Peter 2:24, by including the wording *"in His own body,"* he is refuting that heresy by insisting that the work Jesus did was done in a real, material body that was born physically just as any other person (though not conceived as others are).

Trying to force this verse into the crime and punishment mold can also create unnecessary controversy by reading, "*Who Himself bore our sins in His own body*" as an assertion that He somehow took sin into His own body. That conclusion creates some clashes with other scriptures and result in more religiously induced uncertainty and scriptural differences to resolve. We'll get to the details of the real application later, but for the sake of keeping mental questions from getting in the way until then, let's just point out a couple of basic areas that become too difficult to resolve.

If Jesus let sin into his body, then logically the standard assumption of spiritual death is the result. Jesus, I Am, with inherent life, doesn't coexist with that conclusion.

Observation ought to also point out that a vicarious punishment for Jewish Israel for offenses of the Law does not equal the sin itself. Other scriptures explicitly agree that Jesus was without sin. Paul's epistle in 2 Corinthians 5:21 is one: "*For He made Him **who knew no sin** to be sin for us, that we might become the righteousness of God in Him.*" For most believers, it's likely a fine point that makes little real difference (which is a good thing).

For others, it is a sticking point that can cause some heated discussions. The resolution will appear later in this book. So to not take much time for that argument here, other than to keep some people's objections addressed long enough to get to that part, the simple resolution is to look at the Old Testament scriptures concerning the Law's sin offerings that are fulfilled in Jesus.

Looking in a concordance, those Old Testament scriptures say, 'sin offering' or 'offering for sin' when the reference is plainly the animal being sacrificed, and just 'sin' when referring to what it's for. In the original Hebrew, however, two-thirds of the 960 places where the word 'offering' appears, there is no separate Hebrew word for offering, so that the context determined whether the definition was 'sin' or the animal 'offering.' In other words, 2 Corinthians 5:21 is one of those places where the Hebrew was translated literally and should have been translated idiomatically as, *"For He made Him who knew no sin to be sin [offering] for us..."* (Some other similar New Testament scriptures that were translated idiomatically are Ephesians 5:2 and Hebrews 10:8, 10, 11, 14, 18.)

Similarly, something in Isaiah's passage is also bypassed by making the standard universal crime and punishment assumption. Focus on the following bold highlighted text, just reading what it says (instead of what religion assumes it says), and we take a step toward clarifying my point:

> **He is** despised and **rejected by men,**
> A Man of sorrows and acquainted with grief.
> And **we hid,** as it were, our faces **from Him;**
> He was despised, and **we did not esteem Him.**
> Surely He has borne our griefs
> And carried our sorrows;
> **Yet we esteemed Him** stricken,
> **Smitten of God** and afflicted.
> **But** He was wounded for our transgressions,
> He was bruised for our iniquities;
> The chastisement for our peace was upon Him,
> And by His stripes we are healed. Vv. 3-5

Grammatically, that word 'but' is something that stands out as a big flag. 'But' means that whatever was said just before it is being contrasted with what follows. By example, if I said, "I thought it was going to rain today, but—" you wouldn't even have to hear me finish the sentence. Nor would you need to consult the weather. You would know that my expectation didn't happen; that it didn't rain.

The word, 'we' in this passage in Isaiah refers to the Jewish nation who rejected Him (the Messiah) and made the erroneous assumption that God was also rejecting Him. Christian religious thought still makes that false assumption and so squeezes this scripture into the standard crime-and-punishment scenario, leaving the salvation mystery still a mystery.

Second Audience: The Gentiles

> *And not for that nation only, but also that He would gather together in one the children of God who were scattered abroad.*
>
> John 11:52

Even during Jesus' ministry, there were evident indications that the ultimate reach of salvation extended past the Jewish nation. Jesus went to all of Israel, preaching and teaching to build faith so they could receive healing, yet the only times He marveled at a person's great faith involved foreigners (non-Jews).

Luke 17: 15-19 relates the story of ten lepers who asked Jesus to have mercy on them. Jesus told them to go and show themselves to the priests (the requirement of the Law) and they were healed as they went. The story continues:

> *And one of them, when he saw that he*
> *was healed, returned, and with a loud*
> *voice glorified God, and fell down on his*
> *face at His feet, giving Him thanks. And*
> *he was a Samaritan. So Jesus answered*
> *and said, "Were there not ten cleansed?*
> *But where are the nine? Were there not*
> *any found who returned to give glory to*
> *God except this foreigner?" And He said*
> *to him, "Arise, go your way. Your faith*
> *has made you well."*

When He said the man was made well, the Bible uses the Greek word *sozo* (denoting total salvation) in a tense that effectively said, "You were made whole a long time ago." (Tuck that bit of information away in your memory; you will see it has some real significance!) The other nine only got physically healed.

Luke 7:1-10 and Matthew 8:5-13 both relate the story of a Roman centurion's request to heal his sick servant. The centurion, without any covenant rights, would not even let Jesus come into his house, counting himself unworthy, but sent another servant to ask Jesus to but say the word. In Luke 7:9, Jesus marveled at his great faith saying, *"I say to you, I have not found such great faith, not even in Israel!"*

Matthew 15:21-28 gives us the Canaanite woman who came seeking help for her demon-possessed daughter. Repeatedly rebuffed for being outside the covenant with Israel, she would not give up until she got what she sought. Again we hear Jesus commend great faith: *"Then Jesus answered and said to her, 'O woman, great is your faith! Let it be to you as you desire'"* (v. 28).

As we focus now on the non-Jewish audience, we are going to focus on the writings of the Apostle Paul. We've noted Paul's unique supernatural experience when commissioned as an apostle—to carry the gospel to the Gentiles, all non-Jews. Ananias, instructed in a vision to go lay hands on Paul so that he would receive his sight, was a little hesitant, knowing the damage Paul (then Saul) had inflicted on believers. But the Lord told him what Paul's commission would be: *"But the Lord said to him* (Ananias), *'Go, for he* (Paul) *is a chosen vessel of Me to bear My name before Gentiles, kings, and the children of Israel'"* (Acts 9:15).

Paul did so for 14 years before coming to Jerusalem to confer with the other apostles about what constituted the gospel message, who it was for, and what was required of believers (see Galatians 2:1-9). Elsewhere in his epistles, Paul exhibits a certain quality of differentiating his preaching from what the other apostles preached, yet still describing it as the same gospel. In Romans 2:16 and 16:25, Paul terms it *"my gospel."*

By reason of his commission received directly from Jesus, Paul saw himself as primarily sent to the Gentile world, writing in Romans 11:13, *"For I speak to you Gentiles; inasmuch as I am an apostle to the Gentiles....* "

In Acts 10, Peter, by instruction from a vision, preached the gospel to the household of the centurion Cornelius, and was given insight that the gospel was for both Jew and Gentile. That was shared with the other apostles, so all understood that.

Both Paul and the other apostles came to know that the gospel was for all and shared it with anyone available, but they seemed to recognize a difference in their primary spheres of commission. The most important point is to understand the quality that gave Paul's gospel its distinction.

All the first apostles (and thus the Early Church membership) preached the same simple message (Jesus is the expected Messiah) to the same audience (Jews) from the same playbook: the Mosaic Law, the Prophets, and the Psalms—they comprised the complete source for every daily behavior and the reference for recognizing the coming Messiah. When Jesus healed those blind and lame from birth, cleansed people from the dreaded incurable leprosy and raised the dead to life, any person who was attentive to the Law and the Prophets could recognize the predicted Messiah. But once the audience expanded to the Gentile world, Paul's gospel expanded as well.

Part of what made Paul's gospel different came from his sources of information. Since the Gentile world did not share the same playbook (The Holy Writ); they had no recorded body of communication from God to prepare them for the Savior. They needed something more than just the playbook; they needed the 'how' and 'why' behind the Law and Prophets, which is what we find in the epistles to the churches.

The difference between presenting the gospel through the Law and Paul's presentation of the gospel in the epistles might be compared to selling the latest model car to someone who knows what he wants.

The last time we looked for a replacement car (I wrecked the one we had—it was the only car we ever had that I mourned its loss!) we looked first at a new car of the same model; couldn't afford it. We looked at other new cars. We went from dealership to dealership. I compared every feature and specification published, but knew we couldn't afford them. Besides, they didn't quite meet expectations. On impulse we drove to a dealer in a city 30 miles away. After a brief talk with a salesman bemoaning our lost vehicle, he smiled and asked if we'd wait a minute while he showed us something. Shortly, he stopped outside the door with a vehicle he had just taken in trade the day before—the same model we had just lost, traded in by someone who also loved that model and bought a new one every other year. That was the end of comparing features and models—and the easiest sale he'd had for a while!

Selling a car to someone who already knows and values the model and comes to you actively seeking one is much easier than selling to someone who doesn't even know the model exists. Paul had the same situation spreading the gospel to the Gentile world. Not only did he have to go to them, he had to both demonstrate and explain the inner workings of the salvation message to an audience that had no idea why they needed it.

That added how-and-why dimension of Paul's gospel came from his own source—revelation. He testified *"how that by revelation He made known to me the mystery (as I have briefly written already..."* (Ephesians 3:3). And not just one revelation. In 2 Corinthians 12:7, Paul qualified his source as an *"abundance of the revelations...."*

The gospel first preached to the Jews, and Paul's gospel according to his revelation, give us two incremental gospel pictures that generate problems to this day.

The initial gospel presentation, which is the framework of our present Christian understanding, is the 'legal'-based picture presented to corporate Jewish Israel. It is the vicarious crime and punishment we noted earlier in John 11: 50-52, telling us that Jesus was to die *for* the nation. In a word, it is a gospel of substitution.

Substitute justice. Someone 'dodges the bullet' and gets a benefit because someone else gets the punishment. Legality. Applied individually, the message of this legal gospel becomes, "You've been justified if you'll accept it"—you're the same guilty sinner, but legally justified by substituted punishment and suffering. This gospel is the legality-flavored message; remember, an absolutely just God demands a punishment from someone, better if it's the involved party, but that's not necessary.

Here we must pause and recognize a foundational problem with applying the corporate Jewish gospel to all individually.

Paul's gospel acquired by revelation proclaims the believer to be, not the same sinner justified, but a new creature in Christ. *"Therefore, if anyone is in Christ, he is a new creation; old things have passed away; behold all things have become new"* (2 Corinthians 5:17). In fact, many scholars say that the original Greek text points to not just a new creature, but an entirely new *species* of creature—very different than what the legal message yields! That new species of creature is the consummation of salvation that Jesus asserted when he said, *"You must be born again"* (John 3:7).

That revelation caused consternation to the Pharisee Nicodemus, making him wonder aloud (v.5), *"How can a man be born when he is old? Can he enter a second time into his mother's womb?"* Though Jesus explained it simply, *"That which is born of the flesh is flesh, and that which is born of the Spirit is spirit."* (v. 6), it was more than Nicodemus' natural mind could embrace.

More than consternation, that revelation also prompted intense hatred of Jesus from the rulers when they realized the effect of what Jesus said of Himself as the Good Shepherd sent by His Father.

> *"Many good works have I shown you from My Father. For which of those do you stone me?"* The Jews answered Him, saying, *"For a good work we do not stone You, but for blasphemy,*

and because You, being a Man, make Yourself God." Jesus answered them, "Is it not written in your law, 'I said, "You are gods"'? (quoted from Psalm 82:6) *If He called them gods, to whom the word of God came (and the Scripture cannot be broken), do you say of Him whom the Father sanctified and sent into the world, 'You are blaspheming,' because I said, 'I am the Son of God'?"* John 10:34-37

So there is the plain end of the completed Christian salvation. Supernatural conception in such a way that a believer is a new species of creature, a god (lower case 'g' lest we want to feel too self-important).

And after all these years, having it work in daily living is still a cause for the same kind of question that Nicodemus posed. A common observation at some point in most believers' lives is almost always this: Where's the second part of the 2 Corinthians 5:17 verse? Not all things in my life are new? Everything in my life hasn't just suddenly changed. I don't just automatically have miracles happening. I didn't get healed. Life is still beating me up!

Gideon expressed the same frustration when the Angel of the Lord appeared to commission him to free Israel from Midianite oppression—*"Gideon said*

41

to Him, *'O my lord, if the Lord is with us, why then has all this happened to us? And where are all His miracles which our fathers told us about. . .'"* (Judges 6:13). This is the precise question everyone asks when life hits them with tragedy—"Why?"

It has been observed that people rarely rise above their own estimation of themselves. In the legal gospel, which most hear first, the guilty conscience is addressed by God's forgiveness; but the rational person senses the disconnect between 'forgiven' and 'new creature.' With that rational last connection missing, being born again commonly becomes something more of a metaphorical or symbolic thing, and descriptions of the believer usually end up talking about their legal position in Christ. 'Right-standing' becomes the accepted term for the believer's relationship with God. Thus it commonly takes some degree of repetitive teaching and consciously-intended believing to see oneself as a new, born-again creature.

But where the gospel message to corporate Israel focused on Jesus' death *for* the nation (a legal framework), Paul's epistles to the churches asserted something organic—that when Jesus died, believers died *with* Him; when Jesus rose from death, believers rose *with* Him; when He was seated at the right hand of God, believers were seated *with* Him; all accomplished by the act of believing on Him, putting every believer *in* Christ. In a word, Paul presented, by revelation, a picture of the inner workings of salvation as participation, not substitution.

In their day, the other apostles (and perhaps much if not all of the Jewish church) had the same difficulties understanding a participatory gospel. Peter wrote:

> *And consider that the longsuffering of our Lord is salvation—as also our beloved brother Paul, according to the wisdom given him, has written to you, As also in all his epistles, speaking in them of these things, in which are **some things hard to understand**, which untaught and unstable people twist to their own destruction, as they do also the rest of the Scriptures.*   2 Peter 3:15, 16

Those difficulties in understanding that participatory gospel still persist today among Christian believers.

Why were some aspects of what Paul preached so hard to understand? Because standard surface-deep thought, then and now, tries to understand the message to the second audience (converted Gentiles) using the source for the first audience (the Mosaic Law). Accurate understanding will need to include Paul's source.

Chapter Three

Two Sources

The first source (the Mosaic Law) was for the Jews. In practice it was a system of required behavior and consequences for infractions: a legal system of crime and punishment.

As earlier noted, that second source that conventional minds had such difficulty processing was revelation. Yet revelation is what the Apostle Paul lived by.

*For this reason I, Paul, the prisoner of Christ Jesus for you Gentiles—If indeed you have heard of the dispensation of the grace of God, which was given to me for you, how that **by revelation He made known to me the mystery** (as I have briefly written already, By which, when you read, you may understand*

*my knowledge in **the mystery of
Christ**), Which in other ages was not
made known to the sons of men, as it
has **now been revealed** by the Spirit to
His holy apostles and prophets:
That the Gentiles should be fellow heirs,
of the same body, and partakers of His
promise in Christ through the gospel.*

Ephesians 3:1-5

The necessity for the revelations Paul had can be appreciated when looking at how assiduously the Law had to be drilled into the everyday consciousness of Israel. Recall what Paul noted in Galatians 3:19, that the entire Mosaic Law was added during the Exodus from Egypt because of Israel's penchant for unbelief. "*What purpose then does the law serve?
It was added because of transgressions, till the Seed should come to whom the promise was made....*"
For 400 years, every detail of life was specified by the requirements of the Law and its schedule of blood-sacrifice centered festivals. The awareness of the importance of following it to every detail was acquired at a huge cost, and played out in the years of subjugation, exile, and physical destruction at the hands of Gentile nations.

The central place of the Law, within the history of Israel by the time Jesus arrived, can also be gauged by the proportion of the Old Testament it occupies—except for Genesis and Job, the rest of the Old Testament (the Law and all the Prophets) was written within that 400-year time frame.

People tend to remember and act on most recent memory and experience, especially if it involves trauma. After 400 years of trauma (foreign subjugation, exile, destruction of Jerusalem and the Temple), many were expectantly waiting for the Messiah (the intended result). However, the resulting concentration on individuals fulfilling every requirement of the Law (and even adding some just for good measure) made it possible to see the Law as the base for salvation. The fact that the Law was only added to the original ground for salvation given to Adam had faded, and the previous 3,600 years fell off of the Israelites' mental radar.

Freeing the present-day salvation message from those limitations is the primary objective of this book, and we can accomplish that by seeing what's behind Paul's second point in Galatians 3:19. All of the underlying operation of salvation relies, not on anything any of us do individually, but on a promise made to the Seed (Jesus) by God the Father.

The Seed to Whom the Promise Was Made

The underlying covenant behind both the old and new covenants (made with Israel and Church respectively) was a promise made to Jesus, the Seed, and dated back to the very beginning with Adam in the garden of Eden. God said to the serpent, Satan, *"I will put enmity between you and the woman, and between **your seed** and **her Seed**; He shall bruise your head, and you shall bruise His heel"* (Genesis 3:15).

All the rest of the Bible is detail for that promise.

All of the primary inner workings of salvation depend on the outcome of a 'seed' war that invaded earth that day, a war that started when Lucifer attempted to supplant God. This war is biological and genetic in its visible links, but also dependent on a host of linked actions in the spirit dimension. Thus, when Daniel was given the time schedule of the seventy weeks (sevens) of years that would see the Messiah's first appearance, the crucifixion, and the interrupted final seven years we are approaching, the message refers to that end, *"And till the end of the war desolations are determined"* (Daniel 9:26). War, singular. Were it not for men's faithlessness along the way, everything in the Old Testament after Genesis 3:15 could be viewed as added details for information and omitted. That includes the giving of the Law.

Everything we have come to think we know of God and salvation has been colored by the inaccurate assumption of the legal basis of salvation and the absence of revelation about the biogenetic requirements that reveal the mystery on the spirit side.

And to quiet the mental clamor some readers may be experiencing after reading that statement, let me say something straight up and plain. Just because people through the years have both preached and heard an impaired and incomplete message, it doesn't mean they are not born again, Spirit-filled Christians; it only means that the faith walk for Christians has been harder than it should have been.

For 2000 years, the gospel message based on Old Testament legalism has worked for New Testament believers for several reasons:

- The gospel is what Jesus accomplished in the Spirit, regardless of the beliefs of man.
- Scripture indicates that it is the Holy Spirit's urgings that produce individual repentance and response to a message, leading to belief and salvation. People don't have to hear the entire Bible history to believe, although it doesn't hurt. In practice, everyone is already conditioned to think in crime and punishment terms, so even though the details or

setting people commonly hear in a message may be flawed, it's the Holy Spirit that makes it work. To borrow a math term, crime and punishment is the lowest common denominator of appeal.

- Everyone has a conscience and has offended that conscience at some time in their lives. Romans 2:12-15 indicates that the individual conscience is the ultimate gate for God's judgment standard. Paul there writes that on the Day of Judgment, Gentiles will either be excused or accused by their conscience. This is nothing more than recognizing the distinction the Law made between intentional wrong and accidental injury done out of ignorance.

Here too is an opportunity to appreciate the reality of progressive revelation in the Bible. Progressive revelation simply means that the Early Church did not start out with all the details of the plan of salvation. And since it is *God's* plan, we simply don't know the details until we're told. We can only understand salvation accurately by revelation. For example, the entire Church Age was something no one saw coming, yet it was part of God's plan revealed as the apostles were living it!

We also tend to forget that we are living in the middle of a war between God and Satan, a war that not only embroils the entire earth, but the surrounding heavens. In a war, you don't publish every detail of your strategy for the enemy to hear. Some details must be revealed when the time is right.

A review of history also shows that in war settings, much understanding is impaired or lost, and needs to be re-emphasized, re-explained or even re-introduced to the audience.

Sometimes revelatory knowledge is God introducing the revelation at the right time, sometimes it's shoring up impaired or insufficient information, and sometimes, the audience just isn't ready to hear yet. The disciples had to yield to that reality when Jesus told them there were some things He couldn't tell them yet because they weren't able to bear it (see John 16:12).

Really, the only way Paul could get the gospel for the second audience—the Gentile world—was to get it by direct revelation from God. And when he did, his message added another dimension to the already-existing gospel.

Where the focus of the message to the Jewish audience was that Christ died **for** national Israel, Paul's larger message presented the unique message that believers were baptized **with** Christ, died **with** Him, were buried **with** Him, rose **with** Him and are seated in heavenly places **with** Him (Romans 6:4, Colossians 2:12). Believers are new creatures **in Christ**; even though believers were once in the devil's family, now they are in the family of God (Ephesians 3:15). All those 'with' realities are right in line with Jesus' revelatory statement that believers must be born again.

Believers Become Family

As noted earlier, the word 'for' speaks of substitute justice for corporate Israel, but 'with,' associated with individuals, points to a participation that yields a family link Paul describes as 'in Christ.' And unless specifically used in a metaphorical or symbolic way, 'family' carries a biogenetic story.

The spirit component of that biogenetic story is the mystery we will see, but preparatory for that, one other distinction is necessary to introduce.

Jesus, on several occasions, reaffirmed a scriptural view of humanity; there are only two families, God's and Satan's. When people pass the age of accountability, they like to imagine a third niche for themselves, but there is none. The qualifier for Satan's family is the death that has been passed from generation to generation, resident in the flesh, and that is what every man is by default; it requires no choice.

But the qualifier for God's family requires a choice. If Satan's contribution (and the qualifier for his family) is death (not a concept, but an organic poison spread from the spirit realm), then the antidote is clearly life (again, not a concept, but an organic replacement for the death.) That life is inherently and inseparably in God, the great I Am. Thus, Jesus as God's representative summarized the over-arching purpose of His ministry:

> *The thief does not come except to steal, and to kill, and to destroy. I have come that **they may have life**, and that they may have it more abundantly.*
>
> John 10:10

The purpose of His death was to give life **to** us, and to do so in such a way that the result would be even greater than the life Adam enjoyed at Creation. (God doesn't like to do something halfway.)

In the next verse, Jesus continues, telling us what would be necessary to accomplish that availability of life.

*I am the good shepherd. The good shep-
herd **gives His life for** the sheep. As
the Father knows Me, even so I know
the Father; and **I lay down My life for**
the sheep.*   John 10:11

Most of our commonly-used Bible translations
come via translation from the Hebrew to Greek to
our present spoken language translations. Where
Jesus and the New Testament writers tell us that
He was to give His *life* **to** us (v. 10), the Greek text
uses the word *zoe,* denoting spiritual life, or eternal
life—something inseparable from the person of God.
(If it were, He wouldn't be I Am that I Am.)

When the means to accomplish that transfer of
life is the subject, giving His *life for* us (v. 11), the
Greek text uses a different word, *psuche,* which
denotes physical life: breathing, respiration.

Always, through the New Testament, where the
context refers to giving the 'life' of salvation **to** us,
zoe is used. Wherever the context indicates either
the means to accomplish that transfer or the substitute aspect **for** the Jewish nation, *psuche* is used.
Consistently. No exceptions.

Aside from the issue of accuracy, there is a
practical reason for the necessity of recognizing
this distinction. Without the distinction, a rational

assembly of the picture concludes a side of God that demands somebody die before He is willing to share anything good; yet isn't dying the problem already? We are all already dying! For a believer who made the Christian commitment based on the incomplete, legal crime-and-punishment scenario, the message that "God loves you" is laid over that, but that very real, rational incompatibility gets pushed aside and there can still remain a subconscious reservation that makes it an effort to trust Him 100%. For a non-believer hearing the legal-based presentation, that rational incompatibility becomes an unnecessary hindrance to a life-saving decision.

Why This Distinction Is So Important

One central reality of spreading the gospel involves this important distinction between Jesus' death as punishment and Jesus' death as sacrifice. The only way for people to believe is to first hear; they can't believe or act on something they haven't heard.

> *How then shall they call on Him in whom they have not believed? And how shall they believe in Him of whom they have not heard? And how shall they hear without a preacher?*　　Romans 10:14

If the message is inaccurate, the results will always be, at the least, a little less than they could have been.

For anyone interested in a secondary issue, the life (*psuche*) versus life (*zoe*) distinction has an integral place in understanding what was going on during the three days Jesus' body remained in the tomb. Sometimes, heated religious discussions try to skirt the unsettled parts of a legal-based scenario by posing the supposedly unanswerable question, 'Well, what about everyone before the Law?" Our resolution of the spirit side of the mystery will cover that, but here it's an interesting side-trip to observe that the life *(psuche)* versus life *(zoe)* distinction sheds some light here too.

Individuals are saved by believing a message heard; an accurate gospel message we hope! Thus Peter writes of Jesus during the three days his body was in the tomb as having preached by the Spirit to the spirits of the dead in hell (1 Peter 3:19). Having taken up flesh, the only way Jesus could preach to them at that point was to yield up his physical life (*psuche*) as the means to take the message of life (*zoe*) to them.

As we will see more completely in the details following, punishment for being in a sickened state (the death passed by generation) could never change that organic state. Only the reintroduction of the original life, conception and regeneration can settle the 'debt' and return what God had: "*And the LORD God formed man of the dust of the ground, and breathed into his nostrils the breath of life; and man became a living being*" (Genesis 2:7). God lost a family; that is the 'debt' that is being rectified.

Now that I've pointed out its distinction from the crime-and-punishment view of salvation, let's get more into the revelatory view of salvation as being born again into a new life. And, as with all new life, let's begin with conception.

Chapter Four

The Mystery

I n one of the routines of comedy team The Smothers Brothers, the two are discussing a wedding they attended. One brother says that, after the wedding ceremony, he went to the *conception.*

"No," the other said, "You mean the *reception.*"

"Oh," the first said, "I must have been in the wrong room."

The Smothers Brothers comedy line might seem a little earthy for a religious audience, but let's face it, how many of us got here without some intimate contact on someone's part? When we see a plainly pregnant woman, no one has to ask what happened. Physical intimacy is a fact of life.

I believe spiritual intimacy is also a fact of life, and it is what Paul is talking about when he refers to the mystery of salvation. Writing in Colossians 2:2 of the Church, he prayed:

*That their hearts may be encouraged,
being knit together in love, and attaining
to the riches of the full assurance of
understanding, to the knowledge of the
mystery of God, both of the Father and
of Christ.*

Paul's heart desire is that all understand the details of what God has done in salvation. We could look at a number of scriptures to see that knowledge is not only Paul's personal desire for the people of God, but it is God's desire as well. Hosea 4:6 summarizes God's concern when he laments, "*My people are destroyed for lack of knowledge.*" Even the angels are interested in understanding the details (see 1 Peter 1:12).

The mystery of salvation we are considering here is a mystery because it is something done out of sight. In this scriptural sense, mystery simply means unseen and therefore unknown; not necessarily unknowable. A mystery is only a mystery until the facts are known and understood.

The central mystery to be understood is simply the details of the end of salvation—born again. Let's look at these spiritual details by comparing them to what we already know; the biology of birth.

There are four physical things necessary for an individual to come into existence, and they always come in the same order. Always.

Intercourse. Conception. Gestation. Delivery. No one got here without all four taking place. And no one is born into God's family without these same four steps taking place. Even Jesus went through this process; His mother Mary 'overshadowed' by the Holy Spirit (intercourse; see the definition below), He was conceived, carried full term, and then delivered in Bethlehem.

Because we already understand what these concepts are for a physical birth, let's see how these four concepts apply to individual salvation (the mystery):

- Delivery: The Resurrection and Rapture
- Gestation: Our present development in the flesh
- Conception: The moment faith embraces the gospel message
- Intercourse: The intimate contact through Christ on the cross at Calvary

We will also see the very heart of the mystery, the larger view: that in that experience on Calvary's cross, God made contact with everyone in Adam's bloodline, generating a larger corporate scope that identifies all believers as Christ's body and the Bride of Christ.

Delivery

The Resurrection and Rapture can easily be appreciated as the delivery phase of the birthing process. As a distinctly different kind of conceived being, this is the moment the Church emerges from the veil of the physical flesh, and we finally see her for what she is:

> *Behold, I tell you a mystery: We shall not all sleep, but we shall be changed— In a moment, in the twinkling of an eye, at the last trumpet. For the trumpet will sound, and the dead will be raised incorruptible, and we shall be changed. For this corruptible must put on incorruption, and this mortal must put on immortality. So when this corruptible has put on incorruption, and this mortal has put on immortality, then shall be brought to pass the saying that is written: "death is swallowed up in victory."*
>
> 1 Corinthians 15:51-53

Gestation

With the resurrection as the delivery, we can readily see our present state as the gestation period. As a spirit dwelling in flesh, our mortal bodies are like a womb's placenta that temporarily sustain us, but one day will be discarded. Until that day, we are learning how to live as the new creature Paul's epistles describe.

In 2 Corinthians 4:7, Paul says "[But] *we have this treasure in earthen vessels that the excellence of the power may be of God and not of us.*" And much of his epistles are occupied with teaching believers how to apply that reality in the daily life, encouraging and correcting where necessary. A couple of verses summarize his message:

> *And do not be conformed to this world, but be transformed by the renewing of your mind, that you may prove what is that good and acceptable and perfect will of God.* Romans 12:2

> *And be renewed in the spirit of your mind. . .* Ephesians 4:23

The detailed list of Paul's teachings includes all the spiritual goals and the carnal landmines of people whose spirits are set above, but are still limited by a clinging past and fleshly body. He exhorts believers to live so as to exhibit the fruit of the Spirit (see Galatians 5:22, 23), teaches them concerning the open manifestations of the Spirit (see 1 Corinthians 12:7-10), explains the working of faith and effective praying, instructs on how to keep a church meeting operating in order, how to recognize false teachers, prophetic expectations—these are only a few of the things Paul had to deal with in his efforts to see the first churches grow into mature believers.

Conception

With resurrection as delivery and this current life as our gestation, the scripture clearly pictures conception as the joining of our active faith and the Word of God.

> *But as many as received Him, to them*
> *He gave the right to become children of*
> *God, to those who believe in His name:*

*Who were born, not of blood, nor of the
will of the flesh, nor of the will of man,
but of God.*   John 1:12, 13

*Jesus answered, "Most assuredly, I say
to you, unless one is born of water and
the Spirit, he cannot enter the kingdom
of God."*   John 3:5

*For the Word of God is living and pow-
erful, and sharper than any two-edged
sword, piercing even to the division of
soul and spirit, and of joints and marrow,
and is a discerner of the thoughts and
intents of the heart.*   Hebrews 4:12

Intercourse

Before conception can take place, there must be
intimate contact. This is the part, I believe, that has
been missing from our Christianity. On this idea
of spiritual intercourse hangs all of written scripture and recorded history. If we don't see this, being
born again is still just a mystery and we can, at
best, really be only the same sinners, only legally
justified.

Sensing the necessity of the contact but lacking the clear recognition of the occasion, the Christian message has been plagued, even to the present, with alleged substitution of a physical sexual act during Jesus ministry. It furnishes great cinema for people seeking an excuse for doubt, but the real occasion was in the spirit dimension.

In 1 Corinthians 6:17 we see that *"He that is joined to the Lord is one spirit."* Just as it takes the combination of two physical cells from the contact of two parents for physical conception, it takes a direct combination of two spirits to yield a newly conceived spirit in a born-again person. So, all we have to do is identify that occasion of contact.

Without the Contact

Let's take a minute here to appreciate the negative side of why we're presenting the concepts of intercourse and conception.

Without intercourse and conception, the historical line of thought for the Christian message, with the commonly applied scriptures, is essentially this:

- God said not to eat the fruit; and that if he did, Adam would die. Adam sinned by disobedience, and God meted out the death sentence. With that came ejection from the garden of Eden and lifelong banishment from God's presence. It has been the same for every person since then.

Therefore, just as through one man sin entered the world, and death through sin, and thus death spread to all men, because all sinned.   Romans 5:12

• Everyone therefore is less than perfect.

For all have sinned and come short of the glory of God.   *Romans 3:23*

• Our sinfulness angers a holy and perfect God, who can't even bear to look at sin.

You are of purer eyes than to behold evil, And cannot look on wickedness.
                                    Habakkuk 1:13a

Thou shalt be perfect with the Lord thy God.   Deuteronomy 18:13

Be ye therefore perfect, even as your Father which is in heaven is perfect.
                                    Matthew 5:48

- The universal punishment for anything less than perfection is death.

  The wages of sin is death.....
  Romans 6:23

  . . . and without shedding of blood there is no remission.   Hebrews 9:22

- That punishment is the 'debt' everyone owes. God satisfied his desire for punishment by looking for someone to kill in place of everyone. Jesus was that substituted person and the righteous anger of God is pacified, so we can go to heaven.

Honestly now, an angry God just out to kill someone because the punishment for even the slightest infraction is death in a viciously cruel manner? It makes the average person really want to love and serve Him, doesn't it?

Does it inspire the unreserved confidence in Him that faith requires? Not so much! I think that view of God would tend to make a person want to keep a safe distance from Him, don't you? It's easy to appreciate, with this view of God, that the subconscious of some people could always be wondering whether their latest sins were covered or not, or whether those sins were too big.

Yet the Apostle John perceived God quite differently. He gives us a picture of a loving God we can trust and rely on.

> *Now this is the confidence we have in Him, that if we ask anything according to his will, He hears us. And if we know he hears us, whatever we ask, we know that we have the petitions that we have asked of Him.* 1 John 5:14, 15

Does the rational mind not recognize this inconsistency?

I'm presenting a concentrated summary of the historical Christian message for discussion here. Somewhere in their first hearing of the gospel, most people should have also heard the "God loves you" part of the message. (To hear only the concentrated line of thought above inspires more fear than faith, does it not?)

Remember the difference between the faith that Moses had and the lack of faith that led to Israel's downfall (and the introduction of the Law)? Moses knew God's ways, His character, His personality, His motivation; Israel knew only His acts.

So allow me to point out briefly just a couple of the most dangerous possible effects of this historical Christian message.

The number one issue is that this message presents God as the one doing the killing, effectively making God the author of death *and* (through the cross) the life source. Even when salvation is presented as being a free gift from God, it still doesn't fully address the foundational condition in man: an organic sickness known as death. Thus people commonly still see themselves as just forgiven for the biggest sins to date, not changed in any real way.

I remember talking to a coworker who knew he had, on specific occasion, made a commitment of belief, but still wasn't convinced of the certainty of his place in heaven or his inclusion in the Resurrection and Rapture.

Another visible effect of that underlying historical Christian thought line (and the most common) is the tendency to make faith somewhat tenuous, impersonal, and inclined to stick to staid liturgical forms. One could almost rest the case here with the observation that the most common question from people when a tragedy hits is "Why did God do this to me?" because they have very little faith in God as a good God.

But this kind of wavering is not what gets results:

*But let him ask in faith, with no doubting,
for he who doubts is like a wave of the
sea driven and tossed by the wind. For
let not that man suppose that he will
receive anything from the Lord; he is a
double-minded man, unstable in all his
ways.* James 1:6-8

Sooner or later, the lack of results makes people conclude there's nothing to religion, and they leave church.

Another unintended effect I've noticed is making the expectation of faith into something irrational. Here I'm thinking primarily of the effort to combine the righteous, angry God with the God of love. Talking to people and seeing the volumes of writings through history devoted to resolving that dichotomy, makes me think it is more of an issue than we would like to believe. To resolve it, very often, God is left looking a little schizophrenic, or people just figuratively throw up their hands and say, "You can't know that. It's just a mystery. Faith is just irrational. You just have to believe even though it doesn't make sense."

A most dangerous effect is the false conclusion that, if God punished Jesus for everyone and was satisfied, then everyone should go to heaven without exerting any effort or making any decision. (That line of thought is known as Universalism.) And that belief is an express lane ticket to hell. Jesus clearly indicated on more than one occasion that saving faith requires individual action. The Universalism lie attempts to nullify that reality and condemns people to hell for eternity. Combining that substitutionary punishment for all with the clear statement that all will stand in judgment for things done in the flesh (see Romans 4:10-12, Revelation 20:10, 11-13) makes God's salvation dealings look like a big case of legal double-jeopardy.

And perhaps the most newsworthy effect for today is the open doors that message leaves for cult involvement. Church people are shocked to hear of those who renounce Christianity to declare themselves Muslim and depart for the Middle East to fight for ISIS. "Why would they do that?" is the horrified question. Perhaps they just wanted the attention, but somewhere behind that decision, the Christian message they had been told certainly did not make enough sense, or have enough power for everyday life.

Chapter Five

Contact!

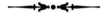

A s we approach the elements of the born again experience Paul calls 'the mystery,' it is helpful to briefly remind ourselves of several foundational issues of Christianity:

- From God's perspective, there are only two families, and they make up two kingdoms: His and Satan's; light and darkness.
- The salvation of humanity is being played out simultaneously on two different stages: the spiritual—the eternal dimension where time, as we know it, does not exist—and the material—functioning totally within the straitjacket of time's forward march, constrained by the natural laws of science, contained by creation, and blinded to the spirit dimension.
- All of this activity is being engaged on three different levels: a *collective association* that

can organically touch all of the human family tree; an *individual level* that gives every person in that family tree the same access to the life offered (while maintaining every individual's free choice); and a *cellular level* that addresses effects on the total person.

- The process of salvation is presented in the likeness of three related events: a wedding, marriage, and conception.

That makes for a lot going on.

If life was a play and we were sitting in the audience—seeing the cross-dimensional links, entanglements and malevolent influences directed towards the occupants of the material dimension—we could well think the material characters so overmatched that the end of the production was already tragically settled.

But we are not in the audience; we are on the stage.

The Spiritual and the Material

One of our biggest challenges in the Christian life arises from the dimensional combination of our creation, simultaneously occupying both the timeless spiritual and the time-constrained material realms.

Life experience can seem much like having our turn at being blindfolded and swinging at a piñata. The spiritual dimension, as the prior-existing and creative source of the material dimension, is the 'real' dimension, so to speak. That's where the whole need for salvation began. Satan injected his poison from that dimension, and God is injecting the antidote from that dimension.

Much of mankind has been led to believe that dimension doesn't even exist, and collectively that's a big problem! Such individuals will have a very unpleasant experience awaiting them at the end of physical life.

Then there are some that acknowledge that unseen dimension but still live as though it is 'out of sight, out of mind', even though the ultimate life-controls originate there. Even within the Christian ranks, many live with such an indistinct awareness of the spiritual dimension that they live far below what God intends.

To help that segment (unaware Christians), I've included here a short dissection of our composite creation.

If we could wield a suitably enabled knife, we could peel back the physical body and find the inner spirit that will survive physical death to experience the afterlife.

For clarification purposes, sometimes the Bible uses the word 'spirit' to explain this part of our being, but sometimes it uses the word 'soul.' For example, in the *King James Version* of the creation of man, it tells us *"the Lord God formed man of the dust of the ground* (the material), *and breathed into his nostrils the breath of life* (the spirit), *and man became a living soul"* (Genesis 2:7).

That can sound a little like a 'ho-hum, we know that' point, but we're building to a key observation that controls everything in both dimensions for us, and doing it without lengthy word studies.

New Testament writers clearly recognize three parts of an individual: spirit, soul, and body. Thus Paul, in 1 Thessalonians 5:23, prays that the *"God of peace Himself sanctify you completely; and may your whole **spirit, soul, and body** be preserved blameless at the coming of our Lord Jesus Christ."*

And even Old Testament passages focusing on the "breath" (see Genesis 2:7) have distinction that seems to relate to the spirit of a man.

Paul also speaks of man in two parts—the inner man and the outer man. In Ephesians 3:16 he prays that believers would be *"strengthened with might through His Spirit in the inner man,"* which implies the existence of both an inner and outer man.

In discussions of this area, there is often dis-
agreement as to whether man is a three-part being
or a two-part being. As commonly happens when a
question is assumed to be either-or, the reality is
both. Clearly the outer man describes the physical
(material or flesh) body, which leaves the soul and
spirit as the elements of the inner, spirit-dimension man.

For closer discussions, we will use the generally accepted definition of soul—that part of us that
includes our mind, will, and emotions.

In Luke 16:19-31, Jesus gave us an after-death
look at the inner man. There He related the story of
a certain rich man and a beggar, both having died,
the beggar going to paradise (Abraham's bosom)
and the rich man relegated to the torments of hades.
The point here is that the inner man has all the parallel abilities we perceive about the flesh. The rich
man in the same recognizable form (albeit spirit)
feels the torments of hell and has the same powers
of memory, thought, and expression (soul).

The question becomes then, "Is the soul something separate from the spirit?" In Hebrews 4:12,
speaking of the powerful capability of God's Word,
Paul tells us that the two are inseparable, yet individually discernable.

For the word of God is living and pow-
erful, and sharper than any two-edged
sword, piercing even to the division of
soul and spirit, and of joints and marrow,
and is a discerner of the thoughts and
intents of the heart.

The observation from this verse is that in the three illustrative comparisons, it takes something supernatural to discern between them.

The secondary focus is his juxtaposition of similarly grouped things—soul, joints and thoughts, compared to spirit, marrow and intents of the heart. A vital tie-in is his inclusion of the marrow of the bone ordered to associate with the spirit. The marrow is where the blood cells are generated, and we will see later how important the blood is.

Some might visualize the spirit and soul of man as two mixed or layered elements. I find it more understandable that the spirit being is the formed substance of the inner man, and the soul is the faculties or capabilities of the inner man.

As I see it, a good visualization of the concept of a whole man might be a computer. We see the outer case with its places to plug in outputs and inputs (like the body), but the real computer—the motherboard—is actually contained inside (like the spirit).

And for complete operation, a computer has to have an operating system (like the soul) with memory and reasoning ability, and interface awareness (the mind passing information between the body and the spirit via mind/brain interface.)

The primary point to appreciate from this analogy is that the mind (processing faculty) and the will (decision faculties of the soul) are the gate-keepers for both the inner and outer man. Nothing gets through without the action (or in some cases, inaction) of the mind and will. They are the referees that either voice or deny faith.

In our next chapter, we will get to the elements of the mystery, but here the take-away awareness should be this. The death-poison that Satan intro-duced came from the spirit dimension and is, from our material perspective, permanent and passed from generation to generation by physical genetic inheritance. Thus it currently resides in the flesh. But the mind and will have a say as to whether that poison continues to the spirit.

A picture being worth a thousand words, I'll include one example here on the importance of that creation reality before we go on.

An experienced minister I studied under, now home in heaven, had several occasions during his life when Jesus, in visions, appeared and, sometimes at length, instructed him on a variety of subjects. In one vision, the Lord spoke to him about a woman exhibiting some degree of mental instability who had asked that this minister pray for her. The Lord told him that neither of them (both the minister and Jesus) could help the woman because she didn't really want to address the root problem. Then, in the vision, Jesus showed him a view of the woman with a demon sitting on her shoulder and talking in her ear, telling her how important she was and how she was unappreciated by others. In the vision, those words appeared as black clouds entering her head, and as she entertained them, she suddenly became like clear glass. The minister watched the black cloud in her head descend downward into her heart (spirit), and from that moment there was nothing anyone could do because she had made her choice.

Forgiveness

In the approaching chapter we will be seeing elements that show God's organic cure for a hereditary biogenetic pathogen (death), which brings about salvation. But because of the important aspects of our soul's control, we need to pause here and address another matter that may cause some objections in the minds of some if left unaddressed.

Forgiveness is a concept almost universally understood in a legal context, and it is central to the salvation dialog. When Jesus healed to show that He was the Son of Man and had the authority to forgive (see Matthew 9:5, Mark 2:9, Luke 5:23), He dropped a bombshell on the Pharisees. After his resurrection, He expressed to believers their ability to bind (retain) and loose (forgive) sins as well: "*If you forgive the sins of any, they are forgiven them; if you retain the sins of any, they are retained*" (John 20:23). That's a rather big responsibility to wield.

Jesus forgave people on a number of occasions, but He did it, not as the end of salvation, but as the action that removed attachments that kept them from God's mercy and grace.

Jesus said to leave offerings and first resolve any issues with others if the offering was to be accepted (see Matthew 5:23-24). Peter wrote to husbands and wives to give each the respect due lest their prayers be hindered (see 1 Peter 3:7). Healing as a direct result of Jesus' forgiveness shows that many of the material things we perceive get attached from the spiritual realm (Satan is the ultimate source of all sicknesses), and I use the word 'attached' deliberately. The Greek and Hebrew Lexicon definitions for the words translated 'forgive' or 'loose' or 'remit' all have the sense of removing or cutting something attached. Similarly, definitions for the words translated 'retain' or 'impute' center on the concept of attachment.

A good illustrative picture of what I'm getting at would be one of the big inflatable games, an inclined track, where a person gets in a harness attached to an elastic band that is fastened to a stationary post. Then the person tries to run up the inclined length of the game against the force of that elastic band. Not many make it.

All the hindrances people experience—whether interferences from spiritual entities or just bad attitudes held tight—are like those elastic bands and get in the way of progress if they are unresolved. It's also like a trapeze artist jumping from one trapeze to another to reach a distant platform—he can't grab the second one that will get him to his objective without letting go of the first. We have to release those things that keep us attached to the past. We have to forgive.

The Collective, Individual, and Cellular Levels

When focusing on the levels—collective, individual and cellular—the main thing to appreciate is the scope God had to successfully address for a complete salvation solution. Every member of Adam's family tree had to be included for direct touch while preserving individual choice, protecting every individual until he or she could make that final choice, and still guarding man's genetic DNA from an enemy attack.

The one thing that brings all three levels into clear relationship is the element we noted from Hebrews 4:12: blood. Blood is the element that connects everyone genetically while giving access to the individual spirit.

Everyone has likely seen a commercial or some visual presentation using the photographic device of zooming out from some physical detail on a person to see the whole person, then a building, the block, the city, the country, and then the world. The scale of salvation is simply the relative position in the blood, zoomed out to include the whole family tree, or in, to focus on the individual Christian, and then the micro-details of a cell's DNA.

Events

The events—wedding, marriage, and conception—give us the procession of the salvation mystery. The three form a succession of revelatory views of salvation—the external ceremony, the relation-ship of total love and trust, and the hidden product of love's union.

Taken together, the three also present a picture of, not only the original Creation, but also God's restored order, both corporate and individual. At Creation, Genesis 1:27-28 give us a succinct sum-mary of original purpose:

> *So God created man in His own image;*
> *in the image of God He created* **him;**
> *male and female He created* **them.**
> *Then God* **blessed them,** *and God said*
> *to them,* **"Be fruitful and multiply.**..."

Blessing speaks of an open ceremony of recog-nition and approval. Created as 'him' acknowledges the individual man and woman, yet looks to the complete 'them' for the perfect complement. The commission to be fruitful and multiply echoes the reality of a perfect complementary pair.

Thus Paul in his epistle to the Ephesians, spends most of the fifth chapter comparing the similar rela-tionships of Jesus and the church to a husband and wife, summarizing: *"This is a great mystery, but I speak concerning Christ and the church"* (v. 32).

In Revelation 19:6-9, we are treated to a view of the final wedding ceremony in heaven, joining the corporate body into a single individual in its description of *"His wife"* (v. 7) arrayed in fine linen which is *"the righteous acts of the saints"* (v. 8).

In Matthew 22; 2, Jesus explicitly characterized God's plan of salvation as a marriage organized by the Father for his Son:

> *And Jesus answered and spoke to them again by parables and said: "The kingdom of heaven is like a certain king who arranged a marriage for his son, and sent out servants to call those who were invited to the wedding....."*

Approaching His active ministry, Jesus revealed the thrust of His work when He and His disciples were invited to a wedding party in Cana of Galilee, along with His mother in John 2:1-11. When the host ran out of wine, Mary brought the matter to Jesus, but He said to her, *"Woman, what does your concern have to do with Me? My hour has not yet come"* (v. 4). Yet He could not refuse the pull of love and faith as Mary simply said to the servants, *"Whatever He says to you, do it"* (v. 5) and walked away to tend to other things. I can picture Him with an appreciating hint of a smile as He told the servants to fill several pots with water that became the best quality wine.

Continuing, we see the marriage practices of the day exhibited.

When seeking a bride, the man or his delegated representative went with gifts, usually including gold jewelry, to entreat both the prospective bride and her family. (See Abraham's procurement of a bride for his son Isaac in Genesis 24 and also the example of Ruth, the prophetic type of the Gentile bride.) Having assented to be wed, the bride donned the gifts and exchanged a vow of intent. At that point they were considered betrothed or engaged but not yet married, and the groom would leave to return to his father's house to prepare a place for them in the family dwelling, the woman awaiting his return to take her to the newly prepared house for the wedding party and consummation.

The delegated agent sent to seek a worthy bride is evident as the Holy Spirit. We can also see the Holy Spirit as the gifts that the groom brings. First, he is characterized as the 'new wine' poured out on the church in the upper room (see Mathew 9:17, Mark 2:22, Luke 5:3-39, Acts 2:13). Then He is the one who dispenses ministerial gifts that God gave men with Jesus' Resurrection (see Ephesians

4:8-11), the One who operates the manifestations of the Spirit (see 1 Corinthians 12:7-11) and the gift that produces the fruit of the Spirit in our own individual spirits (see Galatians 5:22, 23).

Then there is Jesus' reassurance to his disciples, recorded in John 14:1-3, that He was departing to prepare a place for them in His Father's house and would personally return to receive them (the Resurrection and Rapture) to remain with Him always. This clearly places Him as the Groom. And the parable of the ten virgins (see Matthew 25:1-13), though presented in context as a caution to maintain focus and responsibility, is nonetheless a clear picture of a bride waiting for the groom's imminent arrival at midnight (the customary time for wedding ceremonies) to take her with him to the newly prepared home.

Family

And finally, a marriage is a change of family. In the words of Ruth (1:16), *"Entreat me not to leave you, or to turn back from following after you; For wherever you go, I will go; And wherever you lodge, I will lodge; Your people shall be my people, And your God, my God."*

Though not often presented in association with family, Jesus gave the parable of the wheat and tares as a picture of the kingdom of heaven (see Matthew 13:24-29, 36-43). In his explanation to the disciples, the good seeds are the sons of the kingdom and the tares are the sons of the wicked one (v. 38); two families to grow together until the end of the age, lest the good seeds be injured while uprooting the tares (v. 30). Extended to the personal level, think of the tares as the physical flesh body, the repository of death's corruption, and the born-again inner spirit man as the seed God seeks to preserve, possible only by a marriage that joins us to Him irrevocably forever.

In sum, the image of a marriage shows so much more than the traditional legal justification message. The Lord is looking for a bride, an object of love, who will return that love. During His ministry, Jesus met several who were hopelessly entangled in the daily cares of life and remarked pointedly that they were unworthy of Him (Matthew 22:37-38). Faced with that rebuke, a common tendency in such people tends to be an indignant "Where does he get off saying that?" kind of thought. No one likes to admit being unworthy. But the Bride can only think, "Come quickly!"

Chapter Six

Prehistory

I n the last chapter, we talked about the behind-the-scenes elements in life that play a part in the mystery of salvation. Before we go into more detail about those elements, it is necessary to give some prehistory about the necessity for salvation. What is prehistory? It's the rest of a story on the front end: what happens before a story begins. If the story was a movie, then we would call the prehistory 'the prequel.'

We know from the Bible that Satan was once the highest, most important created angel in heaven, and that at some point in the past, he engineered a rebellion against God. The story doesn't appear altogether in one place, so it has to be assembled from the places scripture supplies the pieces. Combining several separated scriptural revelations about Satan gives some of the details.

In Ezekiel 28:11-19, God tells us that Lucifer (Satan) was created as the anointed cherub who covered the throne of God, created as *"the seal of perfection, full of wisdom and perfect in beauty ... till iniquity was found in you."* In Isaiah 14:12-14 God tells us the root of Satan's rebellion, *"For you have said in your heart: I will ascend into heaven, I will exalt my throne above the stars of God; ... I will be like the Most High."* His effort tempted away one third of the heavenly angels (Revelation 12:4).We don't know the exact time this happened, but the scriptural indications are that the result was an earth left in chaos to the point of requiring the six-days of Genesis Creation to restore it.

In Jeremiah 4 we find reference to the cities of the earth having been destroyed (if so it must have been before Genesis since there were none at the six-day events of Creation) and the earth being turned upside-down and plunged into darkness. And in Genesis 1:1-4 we find:

"In the beginning (the original creation out of nothing) *God created the heavens and the earth. The earth was* (Hebrew tense indicating 'became') *without form and void; and darkness was upon the face of the deep. And the Spirit of God was hovering over the face of the waters. Then* (beginning the

six-day re-creation) *God said, "Let there be light";
and there was light."*

When people speak of the "gap theory" it refers
to those undetermined time gaps that separated *"In
the beginning"* from *"the earth became without form
and void"* and *"God said, 'Let there be..."*

We still experience Satan's ongoing sabotage,
Peter counsels us to *"be sober, be vigilant: because
your adversary the devil walks about like a roaring
lion, seeking whom he may devour"* (1 Peter 5:8).

But the point is that all of that happened before
Adam and Eve's meeting with Satan in the garden.

While we can have an understanding of this prehistory through the Bible (it may be a new subject to
some readers), there was no way Adam could have
known about Satan's hostile presence and inten-
tions. All Adam knew was God's simple command:
"Don't eat." In fact, having no experience with it,
he had no first-hand idea just exactly what was
included with the newly introduced idea of death.

Here, is where the standard, crime-and-punishment scenario gives a flawed picture. Accepted religious thought makes the initial assumption that *"in
the day that you eat of it you shall surely die"* is a
judicial edict from God. However, if it was a judicial
edict, it would make God not only the tempter, but
the judge, the jury and executioner. It would make

Him the author of death, not the Giver of Life. Is it any wonder then that people, hearing that message would like to keep their distance from such a God? Or ask, whenever some tragedy strikes, "I was just going about life, minding my own business God; why did you do this to me?"

But it isn't God who executes the evil and death in the earth. He brings good and life. The author of the Hebrews epistle points out who pulls the strings behind all that is evil and death:

> *Inasmuch then as the children have par-taken of flesh and blood, He Himself* (Jesus) *likewise shared in the same, that through death He might destroy him who had the power of death, that is the devil, and release those who through fear of death, were all their life-time subject to bondage.*
> Hebrews 2:14-15

The death that came to corrupt Adam was attached to Satan, the real person with original sin. By yielding to Satan's temptation, death's infection was extended to Adam and his family tree.

This is an appropriate place to correct the appli-cation of a verse that occupies seemingly universal place in support of the crime-and-punishment-scenario gospel message. Romans 6:23, *"For the wages of sin is death... "* almost always appears in the presentation, but the verse is misused in two ways.

First, the verse always seems to be cited in the form just noted which is only half the verse. Considering the whole verse yields a more accurate understanding.

Remember, we earlier focused on that important word, 'but'? It separates and contrasts two opposites that are mutually exclusive. The complete verse reads, *"For the wages of sin is death, **but** the gift of God is eternal life in Christ Jesus our Lord."* Looking at it strictly from a common sense view, you can see a business relationship—wages are the pay an employer gives an employee. And who do people in the world's system serve before coming to Jesus? Plainly, it is Satan. He is the god of this world, and ultimately, he can only pay his employees with what he has—death.

But God bestows gifts to those employed in His service—life! James 1:17 confirms that only every good and perfect gift is from the Father of Lights! Death does not fall into the good and perfect category.

The second way the verse suffers abuse is by quoting just the first half of the verse, and then immediately substituting 'penalty' for 'wages' in an effort to bind the crime and punishment narrative to it. That practice makes the verse read, 'For the penalty of sin is death.' The problem here is the practice of changing the scripture to suit individual belief. The effort to prove that crime and punishment belief ends with the attached necessity of God as the author of death.

And scripturally, there are some very big flags here!

Remember it is the enemy, Satan, that steals, kills, and destroys (see John 10:10). But it is God through Jesus who gives us life, as we saw in Hebrews 2:14-15.

It is the devil who has always tempted people to sin, not God (see James 1:13). It is the devil who is the father of lies (see John 8:44), the accuser of the brethren (see Revelation 12:10); the devil whom Jesus identified as the father of religious hatred (see John 8:44), the devil who wielded the power of death (until Jesus broke his power) and therefore the devil who was paying the wages to all those in his employ.

God didn't have to hand out a punishment of death; it came as a result of sin, and that is punishment enough. Sin is like ingesting poison. Is the resulting death a punishment or simply the effect of the poison?

And if God was the one giving out punishments of death, why would the devil even be in the picture? If God is the one handing out both death *and* life, people would justifiably always be wondering which they were going to get that day! John's gospel makes the point:

> *He who believes in Him* [Jesus] *is not condemned; but he who does not believe is condemned already, because he has not believed in the name of the only begotten Son of God. And this is the condemnation, that the light has come into the world, and men loved darkness rather than light, because their deeds were evil.*　　　John 3:18-19

In other words, condemnation comes because a person doesn't grab hold of the available resource of righteousness in Jesus. In a very real, organic way, it is a picture of someone with a cancerous sickness eating away at his body while a guaranteed cure sits unused in an IV bag hanging beside his hospital bed. The cancer will kill him, not because he's being punished but because he doesn't use the guaranteed cure.

God himself shows us the underlying medical cause of our condition in Ezekiel 16:6 (*KJV*), when he told Israel, "*And when I passed by thee, and saw thee polluted in thine own blood, I said unto thee when thou wast in thy blood, I said unto thee, Live; yea I said unto thee when thou wast in thy blood, Live.*" Polluted! This goes to the heart of the crime and punishment gospel dialogue's limitations. The root problem of sin is an organic sickness, not a behavioral problem (not excusing the behavior). The behavior is the result of the root. An organic sickness needs an accurate diagnosis and a guaranteed cure. You can't successfully treat what is inaccurately diagnosed!

Knowing the cause of death, God counsels us to choose the guaranteed cure: "*I call heaven and earth as witnesses today against you, that I have set before you life and death, blessing and cursing;* **therefore choose life**, *that both you and your descendants may live*" (Deuteronomy 30:19).

From the very beginning, what distinguished the righteous from the unrighteous was not who was following a set of inscribed laws; It was who had faith (born of love) that in the end, the Redeemer would come and bring the dead with Him to stand upon the earth in a regenerated body. We find this in the book of Job:

For I know that my Redeemer lives, And
He shall stand at last on the earth; and
after my skin is destroyed, this I know,
That in my flesh I shall see God, whom
I shall see for myself, and my eyes shall
behold, and not another. How my heart
yearns within me!   Job 19: 25-27

Returning to our focus on the Genesis instructions, *"but of the tree of the knowledge of good and evil you shall not eat, for in the day that you eat of it you shall surely die"* (Genesis 2:17). I like to compare this to a common safety challenge parents face raising children. At the age of about two or three, kids are all about exploring; they snatch and grab anything within reach. They are also not tall enough to see some of the dangers, or old enough to appreciate what could happen. If a parent is cooking in the kitchen and a two-year-old is underfoot, one of the first things that concerned parent will say to that child is, "Don't reach up here because you'll get burned." Now if the child has never been burned before, he has no real idea what that means. So what is the first thing he'll try? Especially if he can see the handle of a hot pan on the burner!

So is the parent's warning a judicial statement with a threat of punishment, or a cautioning

statement of revelation to an inexperienced inno-
cent? (The child may not fully understand why the
parent gave the command unless he gets a safe
demonstration of the effect of touching the hot
burner, but the middle of fixing dinner isn't the
time for an extended teaching session; safety would
demand obedience.)

So the important thing to embrace here is that
God's statement to Adam was a warning statement of revelation about an imminent danger, not
a judicial edict. Having no prehistory knowledge,
any knowledge about it from God qualified as some
degree of progressive revelation.

And it was a test. In a sense, God was sending
Adam into the arena to be His champion against
the devil, and rather than take the time to explain
all the history and do a lot of training, He just gave
Adam the answer to the test.

Picture a boxing match with the trainer giving
some last-minute words of wisdom to his boxer as
he entered the ring: "He has a 'tell'—he drops his
shoulder before he throws a punch. Just take a step
back when you see that, and he won't touch you!" If
what happened in the garden was a boxing match,
the wisdom supplied to Adam was a simple, "Don't
eat the fruit." Had he followed the wisdom, he would
have won the fight and passed the test.

We see God giving Adam's son, Cain, the same kind of trainee wisdom several verses later, in Genesis 4:1-7:

> *Now Adam knew Eve his wife, and she conceived and bore Cain, and said, "I have acquired a man from the Lord."*
> *Then she bore again, this time his brother Abel. Now Abel was a keeper of sheep, but Cain was a tiller of the ground.*
> *And in the process of time it came to pass that Cain brought an offering of the fruit of the ground to the Lord. Abel also brought of the firstborn of his flock and of their fat. And the Lord respected Abel and is offering,*
> *But He did not respect Cain and his offering. Then Cain was very angry, and his countenance fell. So the Lord said to Cain, "Why are you angry? And why has your countenance fallen? If you do well, will you not be accepted? And if you do not do well, sin lies at the door. And its desire is for you, but you should rule over it."*

Here again, not an edict from God, but a caution to someone offended and angry and blind to a threatening enemy. Unfortunately, this cautionary wisdom also went unheeded, and we read in the next verse that Cain murdered his brother Abel. We have no scriptural indication that Cain or his offspring ever truly participated in the relationship God started with the blood sacrifices imparted to Adam, nor the covenant God later made with Abraham and then Israel; potentially half of the human race, lost in one fit of selfishness.

Organic Cause

And so we come to the root that determines whether or not we understand Paul's gospel message to us: the nature of what happened in the garden. If God's instruction to Adam and his caution to Cain were not judicial edicts, but revelatory instruction to blind innocents, then the unpleasant result (death) is not a judgment from God, but the introduction of the biggest weapon of Satan, our enemy. The biogenetic weapon of the enemy found an opening.

The central revelation that the church must see is that the problem has been death, a now organic entity, not God's need to punish someone. Death is not just the cessation of physical breath. It is, by effect, something more like a foreign virus from the spirit realm that causes a corruption and disorder the natural, physical body cannot counter. The only way out of the infection is physical death. It is the ultimate, ironic good news-bad news scenario. You can rid your body of this infection, but you'll have to die to do it. And unless you've applied the spiritual cure before the moment of physical death, hell will still be the destination, because the root problem was a family association with the enemy, not God's need to punish sinful acts.

Thus, harking back to our earlier illustration of a cancer patient with a guaranteed cure sitting beside him, we can see why the Apostle John wrote, *"He who believes in Him is not condemned; but **he who does not believe is condemned already, because he has not believed** in the name of the only begotten Son of God"* (John 3:18).

And Jesus identified the effect of believing, of using the cure God provided: *"Most assuredly, I say to you, he who hears My word and believes in Him who sent Me has everlasting life, and shall not come into judgment, but has passed from death into life"* (John 5:24).

Change You Can Believe In

We can see from the Genesis account that, after the fall, Adam and Eve's condition organically changed in at least two ways. The first way was, as we mentioned, the introduction of physical death. Adam and Eve were created to last forever. Had they not made that fateful choice, both could have physically lived indefinitely.

According to the Bible, Adam died at the age of 930 (see Genesis 5:5). That means God's perfect creation of Adam's body resisted the destructive effects of death for that long before succumbing. Sadly, each successive generation held out for fewer years as death's hold on the human race extended. Death isn't just the moment of the last breath—all sickness and breakdown of the body is just death by degrees.

When God ejected Adam and Eve from the garden, an angel with a flaming sword was set about the tree of life (see Genesis 3:24). This was to keep Adam and Eve away from it, and perhaps Satan. Some see this act by God as just another judicial punishment. But from an organic position, we realize God was simply saving them from being trapped permanently in that sickened condition. Think of someone in the final painful stages of a ravaging disease, denied the release of death. Not knowing what awaits them, many find themselves unprepared for the eternal results.

The second way Adam and Eve's lives changed organically is a little less clear. After eating the forbidden fruit, Genesis 3:7 summarizes the immediate result: *"Then the eyes of them both were opened, and they knew that they were naked; and they sewed fig leaves together and made themselves coverings."* Behind this terse description are details that show us what was happening beyond the visible.

There are two controlling actions in this verse. First, their eyes were opened. Plainly, they hadn't been walking around with their physical eyes closed since Creation; it was a different set of eyes this scripture is alluding to.

We can understand a little more about those different eyes by referring to a later instance in scripture. Second Kings 6:17 relates that when the prophet Elisha and his servant were in a city besieged by the Syrian army, *"Elisha prayed, and said, 'Lord, I pray, open his eyes that he may see.' Then the Lord opened the eyes of the young man, and he saw. And behold, the mountain was full of horses and chariots of fire all around Elisha."* The horses and chariots the servant saw were not in the material world; they were spirit entities. And when

Adam and Eve's eyes were opened, they saw something that was not purely physical.

Some research into the original Hebrew of these scriptures indicates an additional level of action with the phrase, *"they knew they were naked."* Commentaries point out that the true grammatical sense of this phrase is not that suddenly they noticed they didn't have clothes on, but that they saw that they had *become* naked. In other words, even though they were just as physically naked before they ate the fruit as they were after, when their eyes were opened, they realized that whatever had covered them was now gone. That covering was something spiritual and supernatural.

What was that covering they had at Creation that they realized had disappeared? We could get to the answer via an extended word study, but it's easier and faster to just go to the gospel accounts where we can see what Adam and Eve looked like before the fateful garden choice.

The Bible tells us, *"And so it is written, 'The first man Adam became a living being; the last Adam became a life-giving spirit'"* (1 Corinthians 15:45). The central idea here is that if you want to see what Adam was like before the sickness of death entered the picture, look at Jesus during his earthly ministry; only do it with your 'eyes open.' We see this clearly in one event that was told in each of the first three gospels: the Mount of Transfiguration.

Now after six days Jesus took Peter, James, and John his brother, led them up on a high mountain by themselves; and He was transfigured before them. His face shone like the sun, and His clothes became as white as the light. And behold, Moses and Elijah appeared to them, talking with Him.

Then Peter answered and said to Jesus, "Lord, it is good for us to be here; if You wish, let us make here three tabernacles: one for You, one for Moses, and one for Elijah."

While he was still speaking, behold, a bright cloud overshadowed them; and suddenly a voice came out of the cloud, saying, "This is My beloved Son, in whom I am well pleased. Hear Him!"

And when the disciples heard it, they fell on their faces and were greatly afraid. But Jesus came and touched them and said, "Arise, and do not be afraid."

When they had lifted up their eyes, they saw no one but Jesus only.

Matthew 17:1-8

What the disciples saw as their eyes were opened to the spirit realm, was the *shekinah* glory of God. This was the same *shekinah* glory of God that filled Solomon's temple at its dedication, so much that the priests couldn't even stand to enter (see 2 Chronicles 7:1-2). It was also that same *shekinah* glory that covered Adam and Eve before the sickness of death replaced it. An observer with spiritually opened eyes would have seen Adam and Eve as the disciples saw Jesus on the mount, shining as bright as the sun.

This was the second way they changed as a result of their choice. They had indeed become naked because the glory of God had departed from them. Had He so desired, God could have renamed Adam, and called him Ichabod which means 'the glory has departed' (see 1 Samuel 4:21).

Though the reality of the glory departing from Adam and Eve is not a new assertion, it is one little known because the crime and punishment dialogue did not account for the organic root of the problem.

Chapter Seven

Civil Justice

The crime-and-punishment narrative speaks of a universal punishment as the debt we all owe God because of our general sinful condition. We've already recognized that the vicious beatings Jesus suffered were part of the Davidic covenant and by extension for national Israel, and that trying to extend that punishment as a cause of a born-again conception is totally inadequate.

Even Jesus' death and the manner of death (crucifixion) are not really just elements to satisfy a criminal case when we consider that the entire plan of salvation is really a big 'do-over' for created man. The elements that were present in the first garden seduction—Adam, Satan, temptation (see Matthew 4:1-11; Luke 4:1-13), the tree (see Deuteronomy 21:22, Acts 5:30, Acts 10:39) and death—were also present at Golgotha. Only the second time around,

Satan was the loser and the second Adam the winner, the Resurrection being the ultimate and final 'do-over' for man.

The idea of a debt owed to God is indeed central in the Bible, but not in the criminal justice model.

What is neglected is the civil justice model. Civil justice seeks simply to put right what has been destroyed or disabled; to return what has been stolen. Civil justice is about restitution—making an injured party whole.

This is a point where we must maintain both a focus on the purpose of civil justice and the perspective of God.

The Bible plainly shows in Revelation that, in the end, there will be a time for punishment and criminal justice. The devil and his crowd will be thrown into hell forever (see 20:10), and the unsaved will face the Great White Throne Judgment (see 20:11-13). Christians will also stand before the Judgment Seat of Christ to receive reward for things done in our bodies (see Romans 14:10-12), but not until God's civil proceedings are resolved with mankind.

If a car, whether an expensive one-of-a-kind or one off the dealer's lot, was a casualty of a flood, it could be cleaned so it appeared as it did before the flood, but no car buyer would want it—the flood waters would have penetrated anywhere there was the smallest access, leaving the car as a breakdown waiting to happen. It would be total loss.

Or if you owned an original Rembrandt painting and your two-year-old ruined it irreparably—scribbling on it with crayon, scraping parts off, driving a pen through the canvas—would any amount of punishment, direct or substituted, restore the painting? It would not. The criminal model would be powerless to restore. Civil justice, however, would seek restoration.

But could your two-year-old restore the painting to original condition? If so, the child would be some prodigy indeed! Even given that, the painting would always be repaired damaged goods. Your multi-million dollar painting could never be returned to its original value even if it could be returned to similar appearance.

Adam was God's masterpiece, and Satan poisoned and defaced him, and through Adam, all of mankind, and when we recognize God's application of the civil justice model to the situation, everything about salvation becomes much clearer.

Before Satan's assault, God had a newly re-created, pristine earth filled with plants, animal life, and a son, Adam, made in His own likeness; like Father, like son. And then Eve was added, and God had a family. Everything was good. God looked on it and concluded it was very good. God was ready for children and extended family.

Ah, but that was all short-circuited by Adam and Eve's embrace of Satan's temptations. God lost an earth He created that was good in every way. But the worst? God lost his family—every child ever born who could have grown to maturity and never experienced physical death. This is the civil justice 'debt' that has to be 'paid' before God's criminal court holds session.

Civil justice requires that all injured parties be returned to same or better condition. In this case that would mean mankind and earth restored to their original state of perfection. But Satan could not return anything to its original state, even if he desired to. He has no inherent power to restore the earth to its pristine state. He cannot restore men to the God-breathed, living soul dwelling in the *shekinah* glory of God (see Genesis 2:7). There is no inherent creative life in Satan! He can't restore anything he's disrupted, corrupted, stolen and destroyed!

As Jesus put it, *"The thief does not come except to steal, kill, and destroy. I have come that they may have life, and that they may have it more abundantly"* (John 10:10).

Authority

While we've made special effort to identify Satan's introduction of death as an organic pathogen, we must also include the legal area of authority, since its misuse is what allowed death's entrance.

The origin of all authority is God. He made the earth and the universe; He owns it; He never gave ownership of it to anyone else. But we know He did give a commission to Adam for its care. God told Adam to be fruitful and multiply, and to have dominion over all the earth, as we see in Genesis 1:26-28:

> *Then God said, "Let Us make man in our image, according to Our likeness; let them have dominion over the fish of the sea, and over the cattle, over every creeping thing that creeps on the earth." Then God blessed them, and God said to them, "Be fruitful and multiply; fill the earth and subdue it; have dominion over the fish of the sea, over the birds of the air, and over every living thing that moves on the earth."*

Anyone working in the business world knows the line chart diagram for who's in charge. In practice, it all comes down to who's at the top of that power pyramid. God, as earth's Owner, commissioned Adam be in the authority position—Adam didn't own the earth, but he had ultimate say over the affairs of the whole earth (except the forbidden fruit), much like the CEO of a big company would. God even waited to see what Adam would name all the animals (see Genesis 2:19). Understanding the operation of that authority gives a picture of our world history and the thrust of God's redemptive operation.

Stirring opposition that sought to stone Him, Jesus, in John 8:34-36, told his audience, *"Most assuredly, I say to you, whoever commits sin is a slave of sin. And a slave does not abide in the house forever, but a son abides forever. Therefore if the Son makes you free, you shall be free indeed."* Here, Jesus points to the family-relation authority Adam lost, that had to be regained.

Echoing that, Paul goes to the heart of how authority works in Romans 6:16 (*KJV*: *"Know ye not, that to whom ye yield yourselves servants to obey, his servants ye are to whom ye obey; whether of sin unto death, or of obedience unto righteousness?"*

When we read the word 'servant' there, we might well have a civilized idea of hired help. But the sense here is a slave, as we saw Jesus term it in John 8, not just hired help. In the world, any thought that we are free is at best the velvet glove that covers Satan's iron-fisted rule. In one very real sense, this slavery is like gang acquisition of 'turf'—demand for 'respect' by projection of controlling power over both persons and real estate. Intimidation and respect are the tool and test of power's pecking order.

The authority that Adam delivered to Satan was the same commission God had delivered to Adam at Creation. So when Adam yielded to Satan's deception, it wasn't just a game; it was an intimidating challenge for big stakes: who would be the god of this world?

And with that yielding, Adam made himself Satan's gang warfare slave; Satan 'owned' his body, doubly so since his body was made from the earth. And since the children of slaves are slaves, all of future mankind became enslaved.

Thus when Satan later tempted Jesus three times (see Matthew 4:1-11; Luke 4:1-13), Satan ended playing his trump card:

Showing Him all the all the kingdoms of the world and their glory, saying "All this authority I will give You, and their glory; for this has been delivered to me, and I give it to whomever I wish.

*Therefore, if You will worship before me,
all will be Yours."*   Mathew v. 8-9

To which, *"Jesus answered and said to him, 'Get
behind Me, Satan! For it is written, "You shall worship the LORD your God, and Him only you shall
serve." ' "* (Luke 4:8).

For Satan, this was the pivotal head-to-head,
second round confrontation for control of the
earth, using the same tactics against Jesus that
he used successfully against Adam, only more bla-
tantly. Notice that Jesus didn't dispute that it had
all been handed to Satan. Adam is the one who
handed it to him.

(Also note something else here that represents
an uncomfortable reality: yielding equals worship.
That puts the challenge to all who think it's possible
to go to church once a week and go about their business the rest of the week like the rest of the world.)

Thus we find several places in the scriptures
where Jesus declined or could not do certain things
because He didn't have the authority. On one occasion, for example, in Luke 12:14 when a man tried
to get Jesus to arbitrate a dispute with a neighbor,
Jesus simply said, "Who made me judge over you?"
In the more direct challenge of authority, the religious authorities tried to put Jesus in a position of

either denying Roman law or denying the Mosaic Law with their question 'Is it legal to pay taxes to Caesar?' His classic answer, "*Render therefore unto Caesar the things which are Caesar's; and unto God the things that are God's*" (Matthew 22:21) disarmed their trap. In both instances, recognition of duly acquired authority was the issue.

God is perfectly just and honors His Word. He is not amoral and capricious. When He makes a promise, He keeps it, and when He gives a commission, it is given, even if the recipient misuses it, or worse, loses it to another, as Adam did to Satan. Romans 11: 29 says, "*The gifts and the calling of God are irrevocable.*" Though wreaking havoc with it, Satan's exercise of power over mankind in the earth is perfectly legal.

Then what would it take to get around that authority, both organically and legally? The writer of Ecclesiastes tells us the key opening: "*Then* (at physical death) *the dust will return to the earth as it was, and the spirit will return to God who gave it*" (Ecclesiastes 12:7). Even with Satan's control of the earth and its inhabitants, God still maintained a claim on the spirits of men.

Resolution would require something on a seemingly impossible scale, an elaborate plan on the part of God: It would take another son of Adam—somehow outside the control of Satan, but still a direct blood-line offspring of Adam and Eve, first in line of succession before any other offspring, still living—to inherit that original commission of control over the earth and regenerate all the successive offspring after him (even though, by Jesus' time, they were all long since physically dead). Wow! That's a tall order! Part of the original human genome, yet outside of it! Reverse time without changing time! Start over without starting over! And do it 4000 years after the fact! This would take God doing something supernatural!

Chapter Eight

Blood

Even though most Christians have generally recognized the blood of Christ as unique and valuable, there are very few who can explain why and how. Under the inaccurate crime and punishment narrative, the usually unvoiced conclusion left for its audience is that a righteous God demands blood as a punishment for sin.

The truth is that the rescue of all mankind from the wretched state sin had imposed hinges on a direct bloodline from Adam to Jesus for three reasons: for inheritance right to rule, for biological purity from creation, and perhaps most importantly, for saving access to the spirits of all in the family tree. Everything about salvation, including the right to rule, depends on the reality of the biological function of blood.

Let's start with the organic problem of salvation.
The central point of the subject's focus is that when
Adam and Eve made the fateful choice in the garden,
it first caused them to die physically and then to
genetically pass that death to all their progeny (see
Romans 5:12). We know from Scripture that the
prime organic cause is death. When God warned
them of the effect of eating the forbidden fruit saying,
"for in the day that you eat of it you shall surely die,"
the translations tend to focus on the certainty of the
result. But some Hebrew commentaries point out
that passage in Genesis can be translated perhaps
more literally as, *"dying, you shall die* (physically),"
pointing to, not only the certainty, but a cause and
effect. We know that the cause (death) came from
Satan, and that it has some kind of spiritual existence because it finally will be thrown in the lake of
fire (see Revelation 20:13-14). For our purpose here,
think of death as a virus.

If we look at a passage in Ezekiel, we can see an
overt indication of the problem when we read what
we look like from God's perspective.

> *And when I passed by you and saw you*
> *struggling in your blood, I said to you in*
> *your blood, 'Live!' Yes, I said to you in*
> *your blood, 'Live!'*   Ezekiel 16:6

The *King James Version* of this scripture is a little more pointed:

> *And when I passed by thee, and saw thee polluted in thine own blood, I said unto thee when thou wast in thy blood, Live; yea I said unto thee when thou wast in thy blood, Live.*

Polluted in our own blood. 'Pollution' describes the introduction of something foreign, organic and destructive—a sickness, the death virus, circulating in our blood. This is a picture of our predicament seen from the perspective of God—we, as spirit-beings, are continually surrounded by and bathed in an infected blood. And the extended problem is inheritance has passed that infected blood to everyone in the family tree.

As we continue discussing the blood, do so with this awareness. The Bible talks about multiple covenants, describing written or verbal agreements between parties, some representing additions to an existing agreement. Genesis 15 describes a covenant between God and Abraham. The body of the Mosaic Law was an agreement between God and Israel. All of these covenants included blood sacrifices.

But the element of blood predated all these agreements. Abel, Adam and Eve's first son, knew to offer a blood sacrifice as did his brother Cain (though he chose not to provide the expected sacrifice.) They knew that from direct instruction from their father. The first blood covenant was in the blood of the animal the Lord killed to supply Adam and Eve coverings.

The bottom-line focus here is that, although we identify the written or *oral terms* as multiple covenants, the one *element* that binds and personally connects those covenants and participants from Adam to present is blood. So from a standpoint of salvation, there is only one underlying covenant that touches everyone—the blood of God's covenant with Adam. The blood doesn't ratify the covenant. It *is* the covenant.

To see how the blood is the covenant, let's first look at the general factors that make blood the central element of God's covenant with us.

Life

Anyone who has taken some biology in school knows the basic physical significance and function of blood. Its main function is to distribute oxygen to the body's cells. Without oxygen we suffocate and physically die. Every cell in our bodies needs that oxygen to function—oxygen is the cell's physical life. And the blood is the body's highway to distribute it. Scripture describes that same condition in Leviticus 17:11 when it tells us *"the life of the flesh is in the blood."*

But that is only the first part of the verse, touching on blood's biological function—distribution of life. The rest of the verse, along with its surrounding verses, gives the covenant component of the story.

> *And whatever man of the house of Israel, or of the strangers who dwell among you, who eats any blood, I will set my face against that person who eats blood, and will cut him off from among his people.*
> **For the life of the flesh is in the blood, and I have given it to you upon the altar to make atonement for your souls; for it is the blood that makes atonement for the soul.**
> *Whatever man of the children of Israel, or of the strangers who dwell among you, who hunts and catches any animal or bird that may be eaten, he shall pour out its blood and cover it with dust;*

For it is the life of all flesh. Its blood sus-
tains its life. Therefore I said to the chil-
dren of Israel, 'You may not eat the blood
of any flesh, for the life of all flesh is its
blood. Whoever eats it shall be cut off.'
Leviticus 17:10-14

First, the surrounding verses give us a setting that indicates God's view of blood. There is no indication of a lust for blood on God's part. Indeed, if every animal God created was good, and not a single sparrow falls to the ground without His knowledge (Matthew 10:29), only the prospective saving of multitudes of lives could offset His disappointment over the loss of life in sacrifice. We see God insisting on honoring the life of the animals that would trade theirs for the salvation opportunity of God's family. God is not after blood for punishment. God reverences blood because He reverences life.

By God's direct description, the blood is a gift *"upon the altar"* from God. Gifts are positive things.

Covering

The eleventh verse of Leviticus reveals the rest of blood's organic, physiologic function in the covenant: protection.

Blood is an atonement for the soul. Because the word 'atonement' has acquired more of a guilt association through religious use, a simple dictionary definition of the Hebrew translation is more useful. The word 'atonement' in Hebrew is *kaphar*, meaning covering. The word appears 80 times throughout the Old Testament; 76 of them in the Pentateuch (the first 5 books). In 51 of those occurrences, it describes a covering for a person (or their soul), in six places it describes a covering for an altar, in six places blood covers other objects (mainly in the Temple), and in only three places, *kaphar* characterizes it as a covering for sin.

The common religious explanation of atonement is a covering for sin because God can't bear to look at sin. However, the presence of sin does not affect God. The entire point of the salvation plan is for Him to touch the corruption so he could destroy it while simultaneously protecting us.

Divorced from religious association, atonement as a covering, would be similar to a homeowner putting a big plastic tarp on his house's roof after a windstorm tears shingles off. It protects what's under it (the house) from harmful external elements (rain).

Applied to people, the animal blood of the Old Testament, from Adam to Jesus's time, was the covenant's protective cover of the individual inner man from the corruption present in the flesh (sin). The three times that Old Testament scripture associates atonement with a covering for sin, it does so because sin's corruption is the reason for the covenant's blood—it is the threat. The Old Testament animal blood was God's protective shield. All who participated by faith enjoyed His protection. The blood, covering the soul, sealed sin's corruption out.

If blood covered sin, the participant would be sealed in with the corruption, not separated from it—the very opposite of salvation's purpose. Any Old Testament person who disregarded the animal blood sacrifices laid himself open to the ravages of viral death—that would include Cain, along with any who simply neglected it and all participants of pagan religion corruptions of the blood covenant.

Thus when we read in the Old Testament about God making inquisition for blood (see Psalm 9:12), a crime-and-punishment-conditioned mind looks fearfully for judgment, while His real intent is to cure the viral death.

Another passage shows the central physiological importance of blood:

> *For the word of God is living and powerful, and shaper than any two-edged*

sword, piercing even to the division of soul and spirit, and of joints and marrow, and is a discerner of the thoughts and intents of the heart (the inner man).

Hebrews 4:12

Notice this list of contrasting elements that are inseparable. The *"soul and spirit"* are inseparable (making together the inner man), yet God can discern where one ends and the other begins. *"Thoughts and intents"* from the outside seem the same, but intents (purposes) come from the spirit (innermost) while the deliberations on how to accomplish them come from the soul. And in the centermost *"joints and marrow,"* marrow is grouped with the spirit-related list, while the outer joints (bones) are grouped with the outer elements.

Although marrow may seem unrelated to 'spirit' and 'intent,' remember where blood is made: in the marrow of the bones. And when Jesus appeared to His disciples who supposed they were seeing a ghost, He reassured them by saying, *"Behold My hands and My feet* (see the crucifixion wounds) *that it is I Myself. Handle Me and see, touch me, for a spirit does not have flesh and bones* (not blood) *as you see I do"* (Luke 24:39).

Access

Blood is not only the flesh's internal life distribution agent and the covering for the inner man, it is also the physical element that provides connection to the spirit (see Hebrews 4:12). Access is the third characteristic of the blood. Considering the composite material and spiritual nature of our creation (spirit living in a physical vessel), blood is our native element. To contact us directly for the Spirit-to-spirit, born-again event of the salvation 'mystery,' the Holy Spirit has to do it through blood, just as a fisherman must somehow get something in the water to catch a fish.

That access is the reason, not only why blood *is* the central covenant, but why the blood of Christ is so uniquely important to the salvation rescue. That vital importance comes from DNA.

DNA

The one biological element of creation that, first, makes blood so special, and more particularly, makes the blood of Christ so special, is DNA. DNA is so centrally important to God's rescue plan that we could accurately say it IS the plan!

DNA (Deoxyribonucleic Acid) is the genetic building block in our genes that controls what physical traits are passed from parents to children. It is what physically defines each of us individually and genetically as a part of our human family tree.

Extended examination of the myriad of intricate details of our DNA is a great way to appreciate the wonder of God's creation, but that would fill much more space than necessary here. All we need to know here is the key to the mystery of salvation is the mitochondrial DNA of a cell's nucleus.

Remember, the blood directly supplies every cell of the body, and somehow is a connection to the spirit. Within each cell of the human body is a nucleus at the center, and within the nucleus are elements called mitochondria. We don't need any more of a biology lesson to identify the key.

All of the blood covenant and the mystery of salvation is included in this one biological fact of procreation; while each parent contributes half of the set of chromosomes generating the offspring, the mitochondrial DNA of the mother is passed, intact, to the child.

Your mother carried the same unchanged core of genetic definition that her mother got from her mother, and from her mother, all the way back to the first mother Eve, who was made from Adam.

When Genesis relates that God made man, male and female, in His image, the biological side of that is that the mitochondrial DNA is the physical image of God in us.

The Blood of Jesus

Here we can more totally appreciate why gospel writers traced Jesus' genetic trail in the detailed manner they did. Traced through the male genealogy to Adam, Jesus had the authority to claim control. Remember, the commission for Adam to subdue the earth would have been passed down to all mankind had it not been for Satan's usurpation.

Gospel writer Matthew, after reciting the genealogy of Joseph back to Abraham to establish claim to the promise, finished by making sure that Mary was in the picture. Matthew 1:16 tells us *"Jacob begot Joseph the husband of Mary, of whom was born Jesus who is called Christ."* With Jesus' blood traced through Mary, Jesus had the unbroken biological right to inherit Adam's authority and the uncorrupted biological image for conception. (This is the controlling factor from the flood of Noah's day. (Read more in Chapter 12.)

When Luke covers Jesus' genealogy, he cites His descent from Joseph to Adam while acknowledging

His supernatural conception through Mary in a somewhat backhanded way:

> *Now Jesus himself began His ministry*
> *at about thirty years of age, being (as*
> *was supposed) the son of Joseph, the*
> *son of Heli... the son of Enosh, the son*
> *of Seth, the son of Adam, the son of God.*
> Luke 3:23, 38

Jesus' genealogical right to rule would have been difficult to swallow for any who enjoyed power over others, as the religious powers of the day had. We see that also from the civil authority—Jesus' admission that He was the King of the Jews did not set well with the Romans (see Matthew 27:11; Mark 15:2; Luke 23:3; John 18:33-37). Probably, what really offended the religious authorities was the inherent assertion that, as part of that genealogical descent, Jesus was the Messiah.

One of Jesus' early healing miracles was a deliberate and open statement of his identity as the Messiah, wielding Adam's original authority, and the religious leaders didn't like it! Matthew 9 opens with Jesus healing a paralyzed man by saying, "*Son, be of good cheer; your sins are forgiven you*" (v. 2b). This of course, highly offended the religious scribes

present who clearly understood the implicit assertion of His words.

> *And at once some of the scribes said
> within themselves, "This Man blas-
> phemes!" But Jesus, knowing their
> thoughts, said, "Why do you think evil
> in your hearts? For which is easier, to
> say, 'Your sins are forgiven you,' or to
> say, 'Arise and walk'? But **that you
> may know that the Son of Man has
> power on earth** to forgive sins"—then
> He said to the paralytic, "Arise, take up
> your bed, and go to your house."(Vv.3-6)*

This tracing of descent was not only the open
assertion to the religious and civil authorities of His
right to rule, but also to the unseen rulers of this
world and to their head, Satan. Jesus' true identity
was much more than just Messiah for the Jews.
The larger picture shows us the seed war whose
ultimate winner would be Jesus. In Genesis 3:15
we read God's pronouncement to Satan: *"And I will
put enmity between you and the woman* (Eve), *and
between your seed and her Seed* (Jesus); *He shall
bruise your head, and you shall bruise His heel."*

Jesus' right to rule was validated by male gene-alogical descent and, biologically, through Mary for conception as the *Seed of the woman* spoken of in Genesis.

Satan attempted to quell Jesus' challenge to his authority in at least three places. First, Herod's attempt to kill Jesus by killing all Jewish male children two years old and younger (based on when the magi saw the star that told them of Jesus' birth); second, Satan's direct attempt to kill Jesus prematurely in the garden of Gethsemane (more on this later), and third, his attempt to completely corrupt human blood during the days of Noah. Let's take a look at that last point for a moment.

Genesis 6:1-4 relates that some of Satan's angels, both before and after the flood of Noah's day, mated with women to produce the races of giants. The intent of this ploy was twofold: to so corrupt the human genome that there would be no seed of the woman to wrest world control from, and also to get as many as possible to give blood offerings to Satan, thus cutting off those who did so from God's salvation through the blood covenant started with Adam. Satan evidently succeeded on a big scale; the earth had become so filled with the corrupted human-angelic genetic invasion that God's only recourse was the flood of Noah's day, which only Noah and his family were found worthy to escape.

With His descent back to Adam and the attempts of Satan to destroy Him, we can recognize two other validations of Jesus as the fulfillment of God's blood covenant dating, uninterrupted, to Adam.

First is a confirmation of Jesus as the One to whom the Promise was made. Paul hints at this when referring to the purpose of the Mosaic Law: "*What purpose then does the Law serve? It was added because of transgressions, till the Seed should come to whom the promise was made. . .*" (Galatians 3:19). Under all the visible work of God's salvation we find not a covenant with man—although we are the beneficiaries—but a covenant between the Father and the Son. That is why, when the covenant was to be confirmed with Abraham in Genesis 15, he was sedated in the spirit and saw two entities, a smoking oven and a burning torch, walk between the pieces of the slain animals (see Genesis 15:17). Abraham was a witness to God, the Father, cutting a covenant with Jesus.

The second validation happened as Jesus arose from the dead. Matthew 27:51-52, which gives us a succinct synopsis of Jesus' Resurrection:

Then, behold, the veil of the temple was torn in two from top to bottom; and the earth quaked, and the rocks were split, and the graves were opened; and many bodies of the saints who had fallen asleep [physically died] were raised; and coming out of the graves after His resurrection, they went into the holy city and appeared to many.

Now that had to cause a bit of a stir in town! Jesus' unbroken descent from Adam was attested by the righteous Old Testament saints as they came out of graves with new, resurrected bodies. Though Matthew doesn't give us an extended roll-call by name, the fact that the covenant started with Adam means all the righteous from him on took up their new bodies. Only those buried locally would come into Jerusalem immediately afterward.

In our next chapters, we will see the mechanism of the born-again resurrection's intimate entrance. Here though, taken together, these demonstrations of Jesus' unbroken descent from Adam are but the confirmation of His blood as the access highway for the Holy Spirit to contact the spirits of all believers from Adam forward in time (there is no time in the Spirit), whose bodies were, until His Resurrection, still slaves to corruption, but whose names were written in the Lamb's Book of Life. Since Adam's garden choice put Satan in charge of the material world, it took 4000 years of patient positioning on God's part to use that carefully guarded pattern in the mitochondrial DNA and bring about the direct, head-to-head confrontation that would reclaim all that Adam had lost.

And so, that hidden thread of mitochondrial DNA continued all through the family tree of mankind—unknown to the carriers, the use only dimly understood through the progressive revelations from God, and only now examined in detail by today's science—its encoded image of God the object of Satan's attempt at defacement. The scarlet thread pushed forward through time, just waiting for the Author's use—when Jesus arrived in the flesh (generated by that mitochondrial DNA), then died and was resurrected, bringing with Him every righteous believer, those from His day to present, all waiting for what we know as the Rapture.

To reduce the operation of salvation to its simplest description, our natural family tree is the result of generations via our blood. The supernatural end and operation of salvation is regeneration via the blood of Jesus.

Chapter Nine

Defusing Landmines

———+>•<+———

On the cross of Calvary, Jesus came to the moment
of intimate contact that led to that earth-shaking
resurrection of the Old Testament saints. Because
it is so vitally important to understand exactly what
happened, and because even after 2000 years, the
chains of sense-based explanation still leave com-
prehension of the gospel message hobbled, I want
to take a short 'aside' to defuse some of the most
often engaged landmines that impair a complete
gospel picture.

Those elements are the Law (and the term, a
law), Jesus as the Offering, and Jesus' choice in
the garden of Gethsemane. The main reason for
including these elements here is that, unresolved,
they typically seem to be the most often repeated
areas where a mental "Yes, but... " reservation

makes a roadblock to clearly understanding Jesus' ability to deliver salvation.

First let's fill in a little more about the difference between *the Law* and *a law*. We've noted how the Mosaic Law was added because of Israel's disobedience after exiting Egypt, and that *the Law* was Paul's framework for presenting Jesus as the Messiah to his own Jewish audience. The Law was the standard of behavior, with prescribed punishments for offences; and Jesus fulfilled all *the* Law. But later, as Paul delivered the gospel to the Gentile audience, he spoke of *a law* in a different sense.

Summarizing the accomplishment of the mystery, Paul writes, *"The law of the Spirit of life in Christ Jesus has made me free from the law of sin and death"* (Romans 8:2).

Consulting a dictionary, a law also exists both as a matter of cause and effect, and of absolute inflexible constant condition. That is the sense that all of science and the empirical method relies on. It recognizes a given order in the material world that allows us to test effects, deduce the cause, and extrapolate for other conditions.

We are familiar with the law of gravity. You can rely on it. It is predictable. If you step off a tall building, you know what's going to happen.

It is this sense that is foundationally important to bear in mind as we continue. Referring to Romans 8:2 above, two laws are compared, the law of the Spirit of life (the Greek word *zoe*; see our earlier distinction about spiritual life, *zoe*, and physical life, *psuche*) in Christ Jesus, and the law of sin and death. Both are certainties. Both yield their respective causes and effects; sin always causes death (sickness is just death by degrees). Choosing Jesus yields life, because there is neither sin nor death in Him (for another of those "Yes, but. . . " reservations, in Hebrews 2:9, He only *tasted* death for every man).

The reason that it is important to bear this in mind will come into sharper focus when we get to that pivotal moment at Calvary when scripture records Jesus' words, "My God, My God why have you forsaken me?" Religious explanation sees in those words spiritual death for Jesus. Yet if it is a law that there is, has been, and always will be spiritual life in Christ Jesus, something in the religious explanation is lacking.

A second potential area that could hinder understanding of the key moment of the mystery is having a flawed understanding of Jesus and the Old Testament sacrifices. We know He is the personification of those sacrifices all the way back to Adam. The area I want settled in the reader's mind is the Old Testament sin offerings. There were a number of differently characterized sacrifices under the Law. The sin offering was one of them. The crime-and-punishment perspective has always had problems resolving Jesus' absence of sin and His identity as the sin offering.

Remembering the sense of Romans 8:2, we can best understand Jesus as the sin offering by thinking of buying a car. If I enter a car dealership, find the vehicle I want, and tell the dealer, "I'll give you $25,000 for that car," I've made him an offer to trade what I have ($25,000) for what he has (a car). Apply that same thought to our condition—a trade— what God has (life) for what we have (death).

The third area that needs to be resolved before we see the mystery's moment of intimate contact is to consider Jesus' commitment to following through on that offering. The way His pre-crucifixion prayer experience the garden of Gethsemane is usually presented is a real hindrance to appreciating the details of that life transfer.

The prayer in the garden is found in three places: Matthew 26:36-44; Mark 14:32-42; and Luke 22:39-46. Everyone is generally familiar with Jesus as three-times he repeated His prayer, *"O my Father, if it be possible, let this cup pass from me: nevertheless, not as I will but as you will."* Every one of us, knowing what He was about to experience, has the first thought, "I can sure understand that!" We'd all be having second thoughts and cold feet!

But the problem is that belief presents Jesus as, at best, an unwilling offering. Yet if the Apostle Paul willingly ran his race, do we think Jesus would not? Four thousand years of preparation and somehow we think Jesus turned into a quivering bowl of fear at the last minute? The same Jesus who calmly walked through mobs intent on killing Him and set His face like flint to finish His course (see Isaiah 50:7)? Jesus, who confidently told the Pharisees to go tell that fox (Herod), *"Behold, I cast out demons and perform cures today and tomorrow, and the third day I shall be perfected"* (Luke 13:32)?

No, I think this usual explanation of Jesus in the garden leaves some holes. As He went ahead to pray:

> *He took with Him Peter, and the two sons of Zebedee, and began to be sorrowful and deeply distressed. Then He said to them, "My soul is exceedingly sorrowful, even unto death. Stay here, and watch with me."* Matthew 26:37-38

Clearly Jesus was experiencing something—something that brought him to the verge of death—but what was it?

To find out, we have to back up to the previous scene. Preparing His disciples for what was approaching, He concluded the Last Supper by telling them:

> *I will no longer talk much with you, for the ruler of this world is coming, and he has nothing in Me. But that the world may know that I love the Father, and as the Father gave me commandment, so I do. Arise, let us go from here.*
>
> John 14:30-31

When Jesus went down to the garden of Gethsemane, Jesus was expecting another head-to-head confrontation with the ruler of this world, Satan. His first confrontation was in the wilderness where Satan had unsuccessfully tried three times to get Jesus to worship him (see Matthew 4:1-11; Luke 4:1-13). Luke 4:13 concludes that scene by telling us Satan, failing in his attempts, ". . . *departed from Him until an opportune time.*" When wiles failed, intimidation and brute force became the enemy's last resort.

As Jesus approaches the garden with his disciples, he tells them, *"My soul is exceeding sorrowful, even unto death. Stay here and watch with me"* (Matthew 26:38).

We've already settled that He was not afraid of death; and He was set on finishing what Father had commissioned Him to do. In Luke 12:50, He told His disciples, *"But I have a baptism to be baptized with, and how distressed I am till it is accomplished!"* Yet something was trying to keep Him from it, even to the point of death. On an earlier occasion, Jesus told His audience to not fear people who had power to kill the body, but to *"fear him, which after he hath killed hath power to cast into hell; Yea I say unto you, Fear him"* (Luke 12:5; Matthew 10:28). The devil is the one who comes spreading death (John 10:10). He was the unseen one confronting Jesus in the garden.

We then hear Jesus praying three times, *"Oh My Father, if it is possible, let this cup pass from Me; nevertheless, not as I will, but as You will"* (Matthew 26:39). What was that cup? The surface, emotion-driven answer would of course be the approaching crucifixion. But it wasn't the approaching crucifixion He was speaking of—that's what He was trying to get to! Satan was the only one who had anything to gain by keeping Jesus from getting there. Satan didn't understand the details of God's plan (see 1 Corinthians 2:8), but he knew that, whatever Jesus was moving toward, it would be to his advantage to stop Him. If he could kill Jesus prematurely—before He got to the prophesied end—Satan could keep control of the world.

So Satan, unseen by the disciples, threw everything he had at Jesus to kill Him there in the garden. Remember Satan had the power of death. He's delegated it in measures to his under-devils—the flu to one, cancer to another. But Satan threw all of them at Jesus. Think of the effort it would take to resist every known disease at once. And we think it's a major thing to successfully resist the sniffles!

When Jesus prayed the Father to 'Let this cup pass,' it was the cup Satan was pressing on Him. And if the cup didn't pass, He still trusted His Father to accomplish His will, even if He had to be brought back from death to get to Calvary. That is the faith that Abraham had when he was ready to sacrifice his one son Isaac, who was to be his source of progeny. (And the same case could be made of Isaac's faith; he was well old enough and strong enough to escape from Abraham if he wanted). Could He have just commanded it all to leave? After all, He had legions of angels at His command and He had healed about every known sickness in others. Perhaps, but He was always perfectly led by the Holy Spirit. Who of us is qualified to second-guess His action.

And indeed, Jesus' prayer was answered that night.

> *And He was withdrawn from them about a stone's throw, and He knelt down and prayed, saying, 'Father, if it is Your will, take this cup away from Me, nevertheless not My will, but Yours be done.'*
> *Then an angel appeared to Him from heaven, strengthening Him.*
> *And being in agony, He prayed more earnestly. Then His sweat became like great drops of blood falling down to the ground.*   Luke 22:41-44

The fact that an angel was dispatched indicates help against an external obstacle (Satan in this case), just as we find in the Old Testament where an angel was necessary to combat interference to bring an answer to prayer (see Daniel 9:23, 10:12-21).

Chapter Ten

Intimate Contact: The Parts

————⇥•⇤————

S o, finally let's get to the intimate details of God's life transfer. Remember the bottom line Jesus plainly told us in His Word about salvation? He said a man must be born again. Period. Before birth can happen, there must be conception. Always. And before conception, comes intercourse. Always.

Merriam-Webster's lead definitions of 'intercourse' are first, "communication and actions between people"; "connection or dealings between persons or groups;" and "exchange, especially of thoughts or feelings."

We've already touched on the physical connection of the blood and the mitochondrial DNA as part of what happens on the physical side of salvation. The intercourse between God and us (individually and corporately as a family tree) occurs on the spirit side of our creation and constitutes what we call salvation. That intercourse is described in the Bible, but because the Bible uses different terms to describe it, the idea of spiritual intercourse remains a mystery. And, because of the assumed 'crime and punishment' scenario, those terms have taken on only symbolic meanings. That moment of life transfer that happens during spiritual intercourse appears in the Bible under three different terms: *baptism, intercession,* and *circumcision.*

All three of these terms describe important aspects of Christianity. Jesus Himself was *baptized* (by John the Baptist), ever lives to make *intercession* for us, and was included in the symbolic rite of *circumcision* begun with Abraham to gather all his seed into covenant. Christian practice includes these terms because they visibly show an individual's faith and association with Jesus.

But the difference between Christianity and the same practices in other religions is that in Christianity, they are connected to an act initiated by God in the spirit dimension. Because that act has never been plainly described for all to recognize, the Christian message has always been incomplete and, therefore, at least slightly hobbled and hard even for Christians to explain fully.

What follows is the moment that made the work of Christ Jesus a finished work from the foundation of the world. But first, let's fill in a place we skipped earlier.

We pointed out that the Bible is full—from start to finish—with descriptions of salvation (the mystery) in marriage and wedding imagery. But the organic definition of marriage is simply the combining or joining of two things to form one entity.

If you were ever in Boy Scouts, you'll remember that when you are splicing two ropes, the first step was to separate the strands of each end and marry them together with the strands of one rope alternating with those of the other. Press two balls of moist clay together and knead them to form one new whole and they are married; they can't be separated again like they were originally.

Organically, the moment of physical conception is a marriage from God's perspective, a joining of two cells to form a new distinctly different organism. Once done, it can't be undone. The marriage that is the basis of the salvation mystery is a union of two spirits: the Holy Spirit and the individual believer's spirit. This sheds a little light on a much-argued bit of scripture on the unforgiveable sin appearing in Hebrews 6:4-6:

> *For it is impossible for those who were once enlightened* (heard the gospel

message), *and have tasted the heavenly gift* (accepted Jesus as their salvation), *and have become partakers of the Holy Spirit* (experienced more than just entry-level acceptance and have received the full personal experience with the Holy Spirit exhibited by the initial believers at Pentecost), *and have tasted the good word of God and the powers of the age to come* (experienced the fruit and manifestations of the Holy Spirit, including miracles, etc.), *if they fall away, to renew them again to repentance, since they crucify again for themselves the Son of God, and put Him to open shame.*

The point is, since the whole mystery of salvation is about conception, not just a legal forgiveness, a mature believer can't just be un-conceived. God makes allowances for new believers who don't understand the details of the whole picture yet, but for the mature believer who has experienced the full fellowship to knowingly renounce Christ, it is impossible for God to get him back: It's not that God won't take them back, but God can't; impossible!

Such a choice would be a self-inflicted, spiritual suicide. There isn't any do-over for that.

Now let's take a look at the three terms that denote spiritual intercourse.

Circumcision

Circumcision means to cut around. It is a combination of the prefix *circum,* which means "around" (as in the *circum*ference of a circle) and *cision,* which means "to cut" (as in in*cision*).

God placed the physical practice of circumcision as a link to the salvation mystery in the time of Abraham. Paul notes that it was instituted in response to Abraham's faith in bringing Isaac up on a mountain to sacrifice him (see Romans 4:11). The physical action of circumcision became Abraham's (and his progeny's) continuation of the link started with Adam. It involved blood, and we've previously noted that blood is the element that gives individual access as a protective covering for the inner man, and bidirectional access for God to both the spirit of man—for a Spirit to spirit contact—and the physical body—for healing and, ultimately, the final regeneration, all on a family tree scale.

While a legal-framework-gospel explanation thinks of the present physical practice (along with baptism) as a symbolic, foreshadowing type of event, until Christ completed the work on the cross, circumcision was a real link to an as-yet-unseen connection to the coming Messiah, the promised Seed of the woman.

You could well think of the practice (again, along with baptism) like the function of a landline telephone. All I can see from my end is my phone and the connection to the wall; the buried network connection is out of sight. God was calling every person across all history through the blood; faith's action was to pick up the phone on the other end.

Paul dedicated a good share of his writing to his first audience to try to get them past the physical side of circumcision, concluding,

> *For he is not a Jew who is one out-*
> *wardly, nor is circumcision that which*
> *is outward in the flesh; but he is a Jew*
> *who is one inwardly; and circumcision*
> *is that of the heart, in the Spirit, not in*
> *the letter; whose praise is not from men*
> *but from God.* Romans 2:28

It is thus the inward man that circumcision concerns directly as the finished work of Christ. Until the salvation mystery is completed, we are still composite spirit-beings living in a perishable material body infected with a deadly invasion from the spiritual dimension (death). Believers, though, have that invasion stopped at the inner man by the faith and power of God through the finished work of Calvary. They also have the right to exert their faith with the Holy Spirit's power to drive out any sicknesses in the body since it is now a temple of the Holy Spirit in the same sense Jesus spoke of His own (John 2:19).

Viewed as a medical rescue, the mystery process is like a surgery to remove cancer. The first step is to make an incision to access the patient's interior and the source of sickness. Deeper cuts get to the internal site of the malignancy to an extent that the infected tissue can be totally isolated from healthy tissue, and finally removed. Cosmetic surgery to cut around a mole on the skin isn't much of a threat. A cancerous mass in the body is much more of a threat and requires deeper surgery.

But we are concerned with something that has spread through the entire material body in our case. That kind of radical spiritual surgery requires a life-support system in place. It is common practice to have blood available for serious physical surgery. It is also a necessity to have God connected by the blood when the inner man is the target of death, awash in a body circulating corrupted blood.

The entire unredeemed physical body is infected, so from a medical perspective we can appreciate that the 'physical' circumcision that would excise the affected tissue would remove the entire physical body, leaving only the inner spirit-man; literally, a circumcision of the heart (the inner core) of an individual that Paul speaks of in Romans 2:28. That is about as radical a surgery as possible!

Science is presently talking about transplanting a person's head to another donor body as a step to living forever, but God is already providing the complete process that works. The accomplished spirit-dimension process starts with a circumcision not made with a knife, but directly by the Holy Spirit in the blood with the same functions of a physical surgery—separating healthy tissue from infected tissue, and accessing the remaining healthy parts for life-support and replacement of damaged components. In our case, replacement of damaged components will require the regeneration of the entire material body.

We can appreciate the complex intimacy of the mystery further as we consider that it is not just a medical surgery, but a conception requiring Holy Spirit to spirit contact, just as the physical part of conception requires contact and joining of sperm and egg cells. And since conception involves the free-will action of persons, the completion of it depends on receptivity on both sides. God made the initial advance; openness there is not the problem. It is individual decisions on the part of mankind that determine the outcome.

That circumcision of the heart, as Paul terms it, is part of the end result of the individual born-again experience, including both protection and spiritual life.

Before Calvary's moment of completion, physical circumcision was, for successive Old Testament individuals, a necessity to be included in the covenant, because it was an active link in God's larger operation. As we will see when discussing the next two terms, Calvary's moment of completion gave God access to man's total family tree genome. Thus, since Calvary, circumcision (like baptism) became an after-the-fact expression of individual faith.

So in our consideration of circumcision, intercession and baptism as the successive spirit-dimension elements leading to the mystery's moment of completion on Calvary, think of circumcision as the first cut that ultimately opened access to all human spirits in Adam's family tree.

Intercession

This is the term that religious thought almost universally seems to miss, limiting intercession only to the idea of praying for someone other than self. As we will see here, intercession can include that, but in the context of the salvation mystery, there is a primary organic reality that is much more important to grasp. While the idea of intercession as prayer is sufficient for conversational purposes, it is inadequate for understanding the hidden details of salvation.

In the New Testament, several different kinds of prayer are described by different terms. Besides the idea of praying for someone else, what's generally translated in scripture as supplication is what most people associate with intercession—strong, fervent prayer. Desperate even. Loud praying! But no matter how loud, fervent, and heartfelt the prayer is, it's still just supplication. Add praying for someone else, and now it's supplication for someone else. Even though the term 'intercession' is used and even defined in dictionaries as "entreating on behalf of another," it's still not intercession in the redemptive sense. We are looking for the aspect of intercession that describes direct, Spirit-to-spirit contact.

The classic and most important, direct redemptive scriptural reference to intercession is Isaiah 53:12.

> *Therefore I will divide Him a portion with the great, and He shall divide the spoil with the strong, because He poured out His soul unto death, and He was numbered with the transgressors, and He bore the sin of many, and **made intercession** for the transgressors.*

If intercession is defined only as prayer, then Jesus sure suffered through a whole lot more than necessary!

This whole chapter in Isaiah is a prophetic account of what was to happen with Jesus at Calvary. The vital part is to realize that something more than praying is described here, although Jesus certainly did that too. But the praying occurred *before* He got to the cross (see John 17). Something else was going on here.

The central issue of intercession is visible in Hebrews 9:14 as the writer compares the superiority of Jesus' completed work to the Law, saying *"how much more shall the blood of Christ, who **through the eternal Spirit** offered Himself without spot to God, cleanse your conscience from dead works to serve the living God?"*

Here the writer points to the one factor that distinguishes intercession in the context of the redemptive salvation mystery—intercession only happens when the Holy Spirit makes a connection.

For a comparison, that same reality extends to prayer in a way not everyone experiences. Speaking of that context, Paul writes that when we are confronted with challenges so big that we don't even rationally know how to pray, through praying in tongues, the Holy Spirit takes hold together with our individual spirit to interject God's power between the person and the challenge:

> *Likewise the Spirit also helps our weaknesses. For we do not know what we should pray for as we ought, but the Spirit Himself makes intercession for us with groanings which cannot be uttered.*
> Romans 8:26

When people feel the urgency to pray for someone, sometimes not even knowing why, it can be the Holy Spirit's urge. Accounts from people's experiences show that they had to keep praying until they felt a sense of release before the situation was resolved. How many parents with a child fighting on a battlefield half a world away awakened to that urge in the middle of the night until a sense of quietness came, and later found out that it was that moment when their child escaped a bullet or a bomb? This is a measure of the Holy Spirit's active engagement through one person, on one occasion, to directly touch one situation at one point in time.

By comparison, John tells us that Jesus had the Holy Spirit's active engagement without measure. *"For He whom God has sent speaks the words of God, for God does not give the Spirit by measure"* (John 3:34). We'll see more of the application of this in the next section, but here, it's sufficient to point out that the intercession Jesus experienced on Calvary did more than make a connection limited by His then-present restriction to material time. It made a connection that touched all of humanity across all time from the moment Adam yielded control of the earth. No leader of any other religion could do that.

The definition of intercession perhaps speaks more clearly of its connection to circumcision and baptism as one of the elements of the mystery's completion. A word root description of 'intercede' would literally be 'to give' (*cede*) 'between' (the prefix *inter*)—a concise picture of the peacemaker; one who puts himself between warring parties. Or, in an equally appropriate picture, one who sees a person mercilessly beating his slave, and puts himself between them to stop the beating.

In two respects, Jesus did exactly that. The moment He entered the personal physical constraints of the human genome by taking on flesh, He did so as the kinsman redeemer to confront Satan. Secondly, when it came to the moment of the mystery's completion—by the Spirit, and through the spirit-dimension circumcision opening made by the Spirit—every participant in God's blood covenant had the protective and regenerative power of God placed internally between the inner man and the corrupted material body.

At Calvary's moment of completion, in a literal way, Jesus, by the Spirit, extended His hand through time to place it between mankind and Satan to say, "This far and no farther!" During his three-year ministry, He did the same thing as He healed people. Matthew relates Jesus saying, *"But if I cast out demons by the **Spirit of God**, surely the kingdom of God has come upon you"* (Matthew 12:28). Luke has it thus, *"If I cast out demons with the **finger of God**, surely the kingdom of God has come upon you"* (Luke 11:20). Isaiah 53:4, quoted in Mathew 8, 17 sums it up nicely: *"He Himself took our infirmities and bore our sicknesses."*

The *NIV* translation has it, *"He took up our infirmities and bore our diseases."* The *New American Standard Bible* (*NASB*) translation has what I think is the most accurately described picture: *"He took our infirmities and carried away our sicknesses."* Away. To where? Who cares; Away! While the legal crime-and-punishment picture of salvation seems to have always infiltrated that verse, in light of knowing the hidden spirit-dimension operation of the salvation mystery, it seems so much more liberating to see Jesus taking up my (our) infirmities as He took up the comparative infirmity of flesh, interposed Himself between me (us) and the weight of Satan's oppression (sickness and death), lifted it and carried it *away!* What was the moment I was freed from death? The moment sickness had no claim on me?

The moment of Calvary's mystery completion, two thousand years ago!

Having in the Spirit made the access to us (circumcision), and isolated us from the threat (intercession), the final step of the rescue God had in mind, baptism, is the most personally intimate contact.

Baptism

Unfortunately, the word 'baptism' is a term with, perhaps, the most religious baggage attached. Anyone with even the slightest religious background has an awareness of baptism. The physical experience of baptism, most commonly in water, seems to be a part of every religious persuasion, including the occult. It's seems to be the one common element that all religions recognize as intended to either demonstrate or enable contact of the individual with something bigger than themselves through a connection to the spirit dimension.

We are focusing on the mystery at Calvary that made that Christian practice meaningful; the contact initiated from God. And that contact, the object of 4000 years of history with Jesus' incarnation and ministry the culmination, hinged on a baptism. It was what Jesus said He pressed toward.

> *I came to send fire on the earth, and*
> *how I wish it were already kindled! But*
> *I have a baptism to be baptized with,*
> *and how distressed I am til it is accom-*
> *plished!*   Luke 12:49-50

Accomplishing that baptism required something more than just physical actions on Jesus' part. The writer of Hebrews tells us that it was *"through the eternal Spirit"* (Hebrews 9:14) that He offered Himself on the cross; the effective action on Calvary was done in the Spirit, beyond physical sight.

The trouble is that, because they were out of sight, the details of that action have remained a mystery, and have caused the Christian world to take differing speculative views, which have produced unnecessary denominational separations, diluting the effectiveness of the gospel message in the world.

Here then, we are concerned with knowing what is that baptism that Jesus strove for, that was done out-of-sight in the Spirit. When we identify that, we will know the mystery that Paul wanted us to see, and the heart of the Christian experience will be laid open for us all to understand.

As a little history, there are four baptisms that Jesus experienced in the gospel accounts:

1. Jesus' Incarnation: Though the Bible does not explicitly use the word baptism to describe it, Jesus' baptism into flesh was a baptism. He entered our family tree.

Scripture says He took on flesh so that He could be made like us (see Romans 8:3). Keep in mind though, that all that was necessary for Jesus to be like us (though not in the same corrupted condition) was to occupy flesh; more importantly, to occupy flesh whose genetic trail traced back to Eve, as we noted when we followed the blood covenant trail.

As a side note, sometimes, in an effort to present Jesus as 'like us,' the condition of sin becomes the focus, with all the arguments over the place of sin in a sin offering that was without sin. Adam was made in God's likeness, breathed upon as a spirit to live immersed in flesh and blood. Jesus was already God, so assuming flesh within the human family tree was the necessity. The requirement was to be like us, not in the same condition. The success of the salvation undertaking is to find an original seed suitable for the regeneration.

This baptism into flesh can also be regarded as immersion into the collective identity of Israel. (Interestingly, the Hebrew word for 'messenger' is derived from the word for 'flesh.' Thus His incarnation literally made Him the Messenger of the Covenant.)

2. Jesus' Water Baptism: Immersed in water at the Jordan River by John the Baptist (see Matthew 3:13).

3. Jesus' Baptism with the Holy Ghost: Happened as the immediate effect of His water baptism (see Matthew 3:16). This was also an immersion. John 3:23 tells us that His anointing was without measure, so He didn't just get a touch from the Holy Spirit; he had a full-merge experience. And that full experience never lessened, not even on the cross, *"for the gifts and the calling of God are irrevocable"* (Romans 11:29).

4. Jesus' Baptism on the Cross: *"I have a baptism to be baptized with...."* (Luke 12:50). This is the all-important baptism that is the key to the mystery.

To accurately identify baptism, the first thing we're going to do is remove it from a religious church context.

The Greek word, *baptizó* arrived in our Bible translations as 'baptize' and means "to dip" or "to immerse." Complete submersion. Think of it as submersion (or immersion) and no more—nothing religious. When I put my hand in a container of water, it is baptized. When I jump into the swimming pool, my whole body is baptized.

Jesus acknowledged the product of salvation as a regeneration (see Matthew 19:28.) For regeneration, God needed an original uncorrupted seed (Jesus), immersed in the material flesh of the family tree, access to the root of that family tree (4000 years after the fact), and access and contact with the inner man (spirit) of Adam.

Contact with Adam's inner man would require access through Adam's flesh, now controlled by outside hostile forces (Satan). So direct contact with Adam's spirit first required contact by the Holy Spirit (since Jesus was limited to the material time constraints of flesh), and then the contact be made through Adam's flesh, an immersion by definition.

To return to the example of a swimming pool, if the object is to touch the bottom of the pool, there is no way to accomplish that without diving to the bottom; complete immersion is the only way. Until Calvary's mystery moment, God was on the outside of man's created flesh; the only way to directly contact the inner-man for regeneration's conception was by immersion.

In the next chapter we will see what that mystery moment looked like to the physical senses. Here though, let's point out that the baptism Jesus attained on Calvary was not a baptism into suffering as commonly asserted. To be sure, Jesus suffered much to accomplish the end result, but suffering is not what causes a conception. Gospel presentations that dwell on the vicious inflictions of the Roman beatings and crucifixions move people emotionally with revulsion and pity, but may not move people with a sustaining personal faith.

Essentially the baptism that Jesus was expecting on Calvary, that He strove to attain, was a baptism into Adam. That entrance is a spirit-dimension parallel of the physical intimacy that delivers the male sperm for subsequent contact with a female egg to create new physical life.

Thus when scripture speaks of Jesus as the *"firstbegotten"* (Hebrews 1:6 in *KJV*), the *"firstborn of every creature"* (Colossians 1:15), and the *"firstborn from the dead"* (Colossians 1:18), without seeing a direct connection in the Spirit, these references appear as symbolic.

When Paul tells us, *"It is written, 'The first man Adam became a living being, the last Adam became a life-giving spirit'"* (1 Corinthians 15:45), without the direct link in the Spirit, the comparison seems more of a literary device.

With an awareness of the direct Holy Spirit link from Adam to Jesus across 4000 years of time and blood, the similarities—the first Adam who met death at a tree and the Last Adam, Jesus, who overcame death on a 'tree' at Golgotha—are more than just comparisons; they are observations of a poisoned family tree's do-over.

Without that direct link, faith has, in many respects, become more of a maze than amazing, the path from the Spirit of God directly to the believer hidden instead of plainly proclaimed.

For something amazing, let's see how that mystery moment appeared to physical observation.

Chapter Eleven

Intercourse

To comprehend the mystery act of intercourse that produced salvation's availability to all, we must look where it happened—in the Spirit. Remember, it was "through the eternal Spirit" that Jesus offered Himself at Calvary (see Hebrews 9:14).

In the Spirit—that's a term that has different meanings to different groups, and perhaps no place whatsoever in non-religious groups. In practice, most people never have any definite, real-life experience that they can identify as an experience with God that impinges on the senses (no doubt a cause of great sadness to God, since He went through so much trouble to make such experiences available.)

Within the Bible narrative, probably the only people who experienced in-the-Spirit experiences (visitations and manifestations of God) in the Old Testament were the prophets. Moses saw God's back parts during Israel's exodus from Egypt. Ezekiel and Isaiah described their experiences.

New Testament believers are recorded as having such experiences as well, but most of the explicitly recorded instances involve the apostles. When the Apostle John received the contents of the book of Revelation, he was *"in the Spirit on the Lord's Day"* (Revelation 1:10). Paul spoke of having supernatural visions and being caught up to the third heaven (see 2 Corinthians 12:2).

Understandably, some groups have used this scarcity of modern experiences to assert that in-the-Spirit experiences had passed away with the early apostles.

But the reason for the present scarcity of experience is two-fold.

First, God doesn't engage such experiences just to give someone a thrill or a reason to put an impressive experience in a book or to get a million hits on a video they upload to the Internet. He does it for a purpose and for those who are engaged in His purpose.

And second, the simple act of unbelief closes the door to a direct experience with God. Don't believe in direct experience with God? No problem; you won't likely be bothered with any.

So let's look to the Bible to tell us what the mystery contact at Calvary is, because it is plainly related, just universally missed.

First we need to remind ourselves of some basics to focus our attention.

While most people use the word 'substance' conversationally to refer only to describe something with physical mass, substance is the fact of creation we experience all the time, but only half of it consciously. Substance can be material (physical, natural) or spirit (supernatural). Remember the dead unrighteous man who pleaded with Abraham to give him a drop of water to ease his suffering—though physically dead, both he and Abraham had form and substance. Science and physics postulate the existence of other dimensions. Both the material and spiritual realms have form and inhabitants, but our senses can only interact with the physical unless specially enabled by God.

We've noted that as a fact of our creation, we straddle both dimensions. We plainly have material bodies that interact with the material world. We less visibly (but equally as real) are also spiritual beings in the spirit dimension.

Being in the spirit dimension and being in the Spirit are not the same; there is a world of difference between the two. Old Testament prophets saw into the spirit dimension. Recall the prophet Elisha, when in a city besieged by a hostile Syrian army, prayed that the Lord would open the eyes of his servant to see an angelic host of horses and chariots of fire in God's army (*see* 2 Kings 6:17).

Some prophets and apostles were seemingly taken up in visions to see into the spirit dimension beyond earth's boundaries. Ezekiel's experience plainly fits this. The Apostle Paul also says he experienced something that made it difficult to tell whether he was in or out of his body. The Apostle John, relating his vision of the Revelation of Jesus Christ, starts by telling us, "*I was in the Spirit on the Lord's Day*" (Revelation 1:10).

Time is another central distinction between the spirit as an extended dimension and being in the Spirit. We are all too aware of the time limits imposed by the material life, especially since the actions of Adam made death the universal experience. Every second of time spent is a parcel of life gone, never to be regained. Time only moves forward; we get no do-overs here. We can only occupy one bit of space at any given moment, and even the extended spirit-dimension part of us seems bound to time's restraints unless linked to the 'mystery.'

But God is not so limited. He is eternal. He created time. He is not subject to time or distance in the way we are (except to the extent that Jesus limited Himself while incarnated in flesh). The Bible poetically observes, *"For a thousand years in your sight are like yesterday when it is past, And like a watch in the night"* (Psalm 90:4). Peter reminds his readers, *"But, beloved, do not forget this one thing, that with the Lord one day is as a thousand years, and a thousand years as one day"* (2 Peter 3:8).

(For the science appreciator, physics theory predicts that when matter is broken down to a basic enough level, the uncertainty principle asserts itself: it can appear anywhere instantaneously.)

While our senses can be enabled by the Holy Spirit to see things occurring in the sprit dimension (the experiences of the Old Testament prophets noted above), there is a distinctly different personal element with the Holy Spirit that Jesus experienced. He had the Holy Spirit without measure; His body was generated by the Holy Spirit; in ministry His actions were always prompted by the Holy Spirit; and His mind and thoughts were continually a reflection of the Holy Spirit's.

Have you ever wondered what it would feel like to be God, to share His consciousness, His perspective, and His awareness? Essentially, that is a useful way to think of 'in the Spirit.' Every genuine experience with God involves some measure of sharing

His unlimited ability. But Jesus experienced that sharing without measure. Volumes of religious discourse and arguments have been generated over the centuries trying to understand all that He is. But the most important thing here is to accept the reality that, in the Spirit, there is no limitation of time or distance—and that will be the key element that Jesus experienced at Calvary.

To help us organize our understanding of interaction with the Holy Spirit, the Apostle Paul gave some teaching about the manifestations of the Spirit. Without it, we would not recognize the culmination of that all-important mystery:

> *But the manifestation of the Spirit is given to each one for the profit of all: for to one is given the word of wisdom through the Spirit, to another the word of knowledge through the same Spirit, to another faith (i.e. special faith above and beyond general saving faith or the measure of faith that comes simply by hearing God's word) by the same Spirit, to another gifts of healings by the same Spirit, to another the working of miracles, to another prophecy, to another discerning of spirits, to another different*

kinds of tongues, to another the interpretation of tongues. But one and the same Spirit works all these things, distributing to each one individually as He wills.

1 Corinthians 12:7-11

While volumes have been written on the gifts and manifestations of the Holy Spirit, here we need to only summarize enough to relate to the subject at hand.

Paul organizes the ways the Holy Spirit operates when He initiates supernatural inclusion for us. The thing to remember is that God initiates these manifestations. Many have accommodated all manner of chaos and interference from demonic sources by trying to initiate an experience themselves.

These manifestations or gifts include the word of wisdom, the word of knowledge, discerning of spirits (these three reveal something); special faith, working of miracles, healings (these three apply power); and prophecy, tongues and interpretation of tongues (these three are the vocal group).

Basically these operate as needed for the Holy Spirit's purpose, and as far as most people are aware, seem to happen within public ministry-related occasions. (Unfortunately, most never realize that they are equally available for everyday individual use.)

And just because the Holy Spirit may have expressed Himself through a person on one occasion in one of these ways doesn't mean that person has any reason to expect that it should become a regular thing.

The absolutely pivotal thing to retain here is that, while we individually may get an infrequent experience of one or several of these manifestations, Jesus' regular experience included them all; not just seven of the nine. All.

Yes we are talking about speaking in tongues, and interpreting that utterance in tongues in Jesus' ministry. That makes a lot of religious minds quit. For the next scene, you have to accept that Jesus' ministry included forms of both.

Although the usual thought or question would be, "Did Jesus speak in tongues?" the equally applicable, and perhaps more appropriate, question would be, 'Did speaking in tongues and interpretation of an utterance from God occur in His ministry?' And the answer is, 'Yes.'

At Jesus' water baptism by John, New Testament gospel writers describe the occasion:

> *And suddenly a voice came from heaven, saying, "This is My beloved Son, in whom I am well pleased."*
>
> Matthew 3:17

*Then a voice came from heaven, "You
are My beloved Son, in whom I am well
pleased."*   Mark 1:11

*And the Holy Spirit descended in bodily
form like a dove upon Him, and a voice
came from heaven which said, "You
are My beloved Son; in You I am well
pleased."*   Luke 3:22

In each of these scriptures, the previous verse
reads as if maybe only Jesus, Jesus' disciples, and
perhaps also John the Baptist heard the voice.
(Someone else had to have heard it to include it in
three different accounts.) If we understand 'speaking
in tongues' and 'interpretation of tongues' as a part
of the wider definition of Spirit-enabled communication that includes both speaking and the hearing of
the audience, then both were active in His ministry.
The occasion just noted gives us a view of direct
speech from heaven, heard by those present with
Jesus; not the usual experience.

But on at least one other public occasion, there is
no question that other bystanders heard that same
voice, and heard it in different ways. In John 12:27-
30, Jesus was predicting His approaching death:

"Now My soul is troubled, and what shall I say? 'Father, save Me from this hour'? But for this purpose I came to this hour. Father, glorify Your name." Then a voice came from heaven, saying, "I have both glorified it and will glorify it again." Therefore the people who stood by and heard it said that it had thundered. Others said, "An angel spoke to Him." Jesus answered and said. "This voice did not come because of Me, but for your sake."

How clearly people heard depended, perhaps, on how closely they really wanted to hear from God.

Supernatural operation of the Holy Spirit was an integral and standard mode of operation for Jesus; and so we really have to pay attention sometimes to get the full understanding of what was transpiring. (A good way to know whether a scripture was Jesus speaking or the Holy Spirit speaking through Him is to simply observe whether it was first or third person.)

Remember that this whole mystery started out as we were allowed to overhear God's declaration of the seed war's ultimate end back in Genesis when God addressed Satan: *"And I will put enmity between you and the woman, and between your seed and her Seed; He shall bruise your head, and you shall bruise His heel"* (Genesis 3:15).

As we next examine the culmination of that war, the central reality to bear in mind is that the real confrontation was both in the spirit dimension, and in the Spirit, outside of physical sight. It is all-important to keep that in mind if we want to understand what really happened in the Scriptures.

Because of the unseen manifestation of the Spirit, religion has, for 2000 years, totally missed what was happening at the culmination of 4000 years of God's redemptive operation. So let's get to that intercourse, the baptism that Jesus so earnestly desired and pressed toward. (I know, you're thinking, 'Finally! About time!") Two of the gospel writers Jesus record account of the occasion.

By this time, Jesus has already suffered the vicious beatings, floggings, and public mockery, and is now nailed to the cross exactly on the feast day predicted, exactly at the time predicted (the time of the morning sacrifice), exactly on the spot Abraham once offered up his son Isaac, and possibly on the same spot that fateful tree stood in Adam's day. At the appropriate time, the time of the evening sacrifice, He would breathe His last, yield up His spirit to the Father, and physically die.

Between those times, the gospel writers record a wrenching utterance from the cross that, while universally known in the Christian world, has been utterly misread. Mathew records the utterance:

> *Now from the sixth hour until the ninth hour there was darkness over all the land. And about the ninth hour Jesus cried out with a loud voice, saying "Eli, Eli, lama sabachthani?" that is, "My God, My God, why have you forsaken me?" Some of those who stood there, when they heard that, said, "This Man is calling out for Elijah!"*   Matthew 27:46

Mark records it:

> *Now when the sixth hour had come, there was darkness over the whole land until the ninth hour. And at the ninth hour Jesus cried out with a loud voice, saying, "Eloi, Eloi, lama sabachthani?" which is translated, "My God, My God, why have you forsaken me?" Some of those who stood by, when they heard that, said, "Look, He is calling for Elijah!"*
> Mark 15:34

Here again, bystanders heard something other than what was physically said. Knowing the level of Jesus' physical exhaustion at that point, and the similarity of Elijah's name, it's easy to pass over that. But knowing that something was happening in the Spirit, there is more that bears attention.

Perhaps the biggest flag for attention is the assumption of what is inferred by those words—that God, the Father, totally abandoned Jesus on the cross, and that His death was spiritual also, necessarily meaning the complete withdrawal of, and separation from the Holy Spirit.

But recalling John's description of Jesus' unlimited relationship with the Holy Spirit should raise a cautionary flag at that interpretation.

As Jesus entered public ministry, John the Baptist said of Him, *"For He whom God has sent speaks the words of God, for God does not give the Spirit by measure"* (John 3:34). Jesus had *all* of the Holy Spirit, *all* of the time, in *every* type of manifestation, and God (the Father) didn't withdraw any part of that, even for a moment, *"for the gifts and calling of God are irrevocable"* (Romans 11:29).

This evident incompatibility indicated by that scripture is a big red flag begging the readers' attention! Least we dismiss it, consider that the utterance reveals several other inconsistencies that need resolution.

After relating Jesus' utterance, both scripture references give a translation, Mark's writing saying explicitly, *"which is translated...."* But is it translated? Was the speech not clear? If the writer simply tried to clarify an indistinctly uttered or poorly heard speech, he would have said so. Translating is something that is done between languages. The necessity to offer a 'translation' is red flag number two.

Then there is the text translation itself; red flag number three.

The entire body of our Bible is translated into the language of a target reader; English, Spanish, etc. And yet somewhere in the process, the words that Jesus uttered here were not simply translated with the rest and presented as "Jesus said." His words here are kept in the original spoken language, and then the translation added. And that didn't come afterward in subsequent translators' efforts when printing revolutionized public access to the Bible. The original gospel writers put it down this way deliberately.

And what about the language itself? The exact words of Jesus' utterance, *"Eloi, Eloi, lama sabachthani?"* are Aramaic, the common language of the day. Everyone there at the cross spoke Aramaic.

There was no reason to offer a clarification, much less a translation, of something uttered in the language that every hearer understood. That would be like me saying something in my native English to a family member, and then saying, "That is translated," and repeating the very same thing again in the same English. Flag number four.

And the fifth flag every Bible student should notice is the apparent inconsistency regarding His union with God, both Father and Holy Spirit. Sometimes, I think this causes more faith hesitancies for people than all other things combined—it so offends common sense.

Remember the occasion of His water baptism noted earlier when men heard the Father's voice from heaven, "*This is My beloved Son, in whom I am well pleased*"?

Jesus came to successfully redeem all creation, to do and say the exact words given Him by the Father, and suddenly the Father abandoned Him?

Remember when Jesus said, "*When you lift up the Son of Man, then you will know that I am He, and that I do nothing of Myself; but as My Father taught Me, I speak these things. And He who sent Me is with Me. The Father has not left Me alone, for I always do those things that please Him*" (John 8:28-29) or "*I and My Father are one*" (John 10:30), or "*Indeed the hour is coming, yes, has now come, that each of you will be scattered, each to his own, and will leave Me alone. And yet I am not alone, because the Father is with Me"* (John 16:32).

Or the entire seventeenth chapter of John, relating Jesus' departing prayer to the Father on behalf of all who would believe. Here are some relevant out-takes. First he said of the disciples, *"Now I am no longer in the world, but these are in the world, and I come to You. Holy Father, keep through Your name those whom You have given Me, that they may be one as we are"* (v.11). Later, in verse 21, He prayed for all who would believe, *"that they all may be one, as You, Father, are in Me, and I in You; that they also may be one in us, that the world may believe that You sent me."*

Does this really sound like, if everything went as planned, the Father would leave Jesus destitute and alone? And for believers, is our every-moment concern that, if we do our best to do what God asks, we risk rejection at any moment?

Jesus' presentation as Christ Jesus goes directly to His total union with the Holy Spirit. The word 'Christ' comes from a Greek word referring to the anointing—the Holy Spirit is the anointing. As we noted before, the assumption has been of 'spiritual' death, i.e. total separation from the Holy Spirit as well.

If that happened, then Jesus ceased to be the Christ.

The very psalm most quoted to support such an explanation (Psalm 22) starts with David's poignant cry, "*My God, my God, why have you forsaken me,*" but continues in the middle verses to plainly describe the Messiah's crucifixion experience, explicitly telling us that He (Jesus) was not abandoned; "*For He* (God) *has not despised nor abhorred the affliction of the afflicted*" (Psalm 22:24).

And consider the three days He was physically dead and His body in the tomb. What was He doing? Peter tells us that he was preaching to the departed dead, by the Spirit.

> *For Christ also suffered once for sins, the just for the unjust, that He might bring us to God, being put to death in the flesh but made alive by the Spirit, by whom also He went and preached to the spirits in prison, who formerly were disobedient, when once the Divine long-suffering waited in the days of Noah....*
>
> 1 Peter 3:18-20

If Jesus was preaching to the spirits in hell during those three days by the Holy Spirit, He could not have been separated from the Holy Spirit. And if preaching without the Holy Spirit, how did the dead come forth from the grave with Him when He was resurrected?

But the most obvious refutation of this explanation is that His body did not see corruption while He was absent from it: *"For You will not leave my soul in Sheol, nor will You allow Your Holy One to see corruption"* (Psalm 16:10). Jesus plainly told the people to expect His resurrection:

> *But He answered and said to them, "An evil and adulterous generation seeks after a sign, and no sign will be given it except the sign of the prophet Jonah. For as Jonah was three days and three nights in the belly of the great fish, so will the Son of Man be three days and three nights in the heart of the earth."*
> Matthew 12:39-40

Jesus also used the occasion of his friend Lazarus' death to remind us all plainly what normally happens to a dead corpse over three days when Jesus said, " *'Take away the stone.' Martha, the sister of him who was dead, said to Him, 'Lord, by this time there is a stench, for he has been dead four days' "* (John 11:39).

The normal experience of a dead physical body is decay: corruption. But Jesus' body did not experience decay, because He was never separated from the Holy Spirit: He did not die spiritually, which the writer of Acts confirms:

> *For David, after he had served his own generation by the will of God, fell asleep, was buried with his fathers, and saw corruption; But He whom God raised up saw no corruption* (Acts 13:36-37).

Simple common sense rules out the possibility of the Holy Spirit separating from Jesus. The Holy Spirit created His physical body (combining with the mitochondrial DNA of the woman). To separate from Him would have required His body to simply no longer exist!

Having plainly presented Himself during the examination with Herod and Pilate as being I Am (in Matthew 26:64, Mark 14:62, Luke 22:70, and John 18:37), the idea of spiritual death just doesn't fit.

Allied with this is another flag. Four thousand years of effort, with the point being to reintroduce spiritual life, and God moves heaven and earth to get Jesus to that moment, and then withdraws the one thing that He sent Him to bring?

The point of noting these red flags (inconsistencies) is to focus our attention on one thing—something was going on in the Spirit that assumptions have missed, and we want to identify what that was.

Coming back to His utterance and the writers' need to offer a translation, unless there was something notable going on, it should have been a simple matter of relating what happened. Bystanders should have easily understood Jesus' words, and the writers should have had no need to give us the raw Aramaic and then add a translation. They were writing to their own people.

The resolution for the gospel writers' seemingly unnecessary translation is found in the *New Jerusalem Bible* translation, which came directly from Aramaic writings instead of via Greek manuscripts. There, *"Jesus cried out with a loud voice saying, 'Eli, Eli, lemana shabachthani!,' which is being interpreted, 'My God, My God, for this was I spared!'"* (i.e. This was my destiny!)

Jesus proclaimed a triumphant exclamation of success, not a bleak question of hopelessness! Much as the Jews of His day could not resolve the seemingly incompatible pictures of the Messiah as both

Suffering Servant and Conquering King, definers of the Christian message, unable to resolve the clearly polar opposite pictures of the key moment of Calvary, have thrown out the translation that didn't fit the accepted picture, and skipped or re-explained the parts that plainly state the opposite.

Playing devil's advocate for a minute, let's say the two phrases one after the other. If they are spoken without distinct enunciation, isn't it easy to mistake one for the other? And of course, Jesus had to be physically exhausted at that point, after vicious beatings and the cruelty of the cross; isn't it possible that it was a little indistinct and different people heard it differently? That picture totally ignores the 'flags' of supernatural operation and assumes God can't keep track of His own Word, closing the door on the real story, and forcing a decision: which version to believe.

Relying only on the rational, conventional religious thought concludes that only one can be right. Yet the reality is that both translations are right. Both utterances, *'Eli, Eli, lemana shabachthani!,' which is being interpreted, 'My God, My God, for this was I spared!'* and *"Eloi, Eloi, lama sabachthani?" which is translated, "My God, My God, why have you forsaken me?"*, though presenting totally opposite conclusions, are accurately recorded.

Something was going on in the Spirit.

The act of physical intercourse is complete entrance of one into another. In the Spirit, the baptism Jesus pressed toward was the intercession spoken of by the prophet Isaiah:

> *Yet it pleased the Lord to bruise Him; He has put Him to grief. When you make His soul an offering for sin, He shall see His seed, He shall prolong His days, and the pleasure of the Lord shall prosper in His hand.* Isaiah 53:10

So what exactly was happening?

Remember the bottom line: You must be born-again (from on high). A conception. We have arrived at the bottom line: intercourse—intimate, Spirit-to-spirit contact.

The productive focus of physical intercourse is a combination of reproductive cells (sperm and egg) via body fluids. The requirement of spiritual reproduction is traced through the blood all the way back to Adam. The life is in the blood (see Leviticus 17:11), and the Spirit is self-existing Life—biologically, the Spirit has access via the blood of the covenant animals slain from Adam to Jesus, and the

Spirit is the blood of the covenant, having begotten Jesus' physical body.

So at that moment of baptism (total immersion), at the end of that river of blood, circumcision discerned spirit from soul (Hebrews 4:12) and intercession put life between Adam (and all who were still in him; like all the oak trees still yet in an acorn) and death.

By a supernatural manifestation of tongues and interpretation of tongues, we heard the words generated by the Holy Spirit's contact with Adam 4000 years later through two different scripture translations, representing two mediums—physical sound and the Holy Spirit.

The physical sound heard, being translated: *"My God, My God, for this was I spared,"* a statement of destiny's triumph.

In the Spirit, the moment of intercourse's contact, being translated: *"My God, My God, why have you forsaken me?"*—a bleak question of despair.

Yet we know Jesus was not forsaken on the cross.

Who then was speaking?

Having not experienced this myself, the best way I know to show the experience is to relate that of another I studied under.

One universally recognized minister, now gone on home with the Lord, author of a number of books, personally sent as a 'John the Baptist' of Jesus' return, and experiencing a number of interactions in the Spirit, described an occasion when he was in prayer and an urgency to pray for the lost came on him. Yielding to that urge, he experienced a moment when he wasn't even aware of himself, but seemed to actually physically feel, through the lost souls in hell, the burning fire, the thirst and the utter lack of God. In the Spirit, he says, he cried out for help, and something to drink, relief from the burning torment. He was momentarily touched with the feeling of their torment.

That was a moment of only partial intercession. But Jesus had the Spirit without measure. The moment of intercession heard on the cross was full. He was touched with the feeling of our infirmities the moment He took on flesh. He took up our burden of death and carried it away at the intercession of the cross.

It is fully descriptive, not just symbolically parallel, that the Apostle Paul calls Jesus the Last Adam. It is by the Holy Spirit's intercession connection on the 'tree' to Adam that we hear him, Adam, transmitted through the blood of the Covenant.

Now, see yourself as if you were the first Adam. From the moment of first breath, you've known nothing but the intimate fellowship with God. You and Eve were clothed with the *Shekinah* Glory of God. To know what you looked like, someone would have to see Jesus on the mount of transfiguration. You walked with God daily in the garden, face-to-face, glory-to-Glory. You named all the animals; they were more like pets than wild things to be avoided or food to be hunted.

And then, the fateful decision and its consequences changed everything. When God told you, ". . . *But of the tree of the knowledge of good and evil you shall not eat of it, for in the day that you eat of it you shall surely die*" (Genesis 2:17), death was something unknown to you, the object of a perhaps stern caution, but outside of experience. God was not threatening to exact a punishment of death, He was warning you of a preexisting threat. You had no real picture of all the effects.

And now the effects had hit home.

Your covering, the *Shekinah* Glory of God, disappeared, leaving you and Eve uncovered. You had become naked. Leaves were a poor substitute for the glory. And then the Lord God called to you and said, "Where are you?" Nowhere to hide! And you are ejected permanently from the garden! The world had become a much darker place, more so than you knew.

But the fix provided was even more traumatic. The Lord killed an animal to make you coverings from the skins. The lamb you had just named, the one that was like a pet to you—its still-warm, bloody skin is now your covering. Your senses are reeling, there's blood everywhere! Everywhere!

The blood is on you, on Eve, on the Lords hands and arms. The caution of 'death' didn't sound like this! And the Lord standing with the now-skinned, bloody carcass of the lamb in a pool of blood, and the fire coming down from the sky, consuming the carcass and the blood in a deafening rush, and the Lord disappearing in the fire.

And then, the terrible, empty silence!

And you know in your gut that you will never in your life ever again walk with the Lord in the cool of the evening.

And you are left alone to find out about this new thing called death. You will be 930 long years finding out about it before your body succumbs to it.

I think any one of us, in that situation, would indeed cry out, "My God, My God, why have you forsaken me?" It was the first Adam, heard through the Spirit, who cried out, "My God, My God, Why have you forsaken me?"

Senses numbed by the new reality, it would indeed be hard to see that blood as the return to the way things were. That animal blood was one end of a 4000-year bridge to Jesus, the Lamb slain from the foundation of the world (see Revelation 13:8), the faith of God unwaveringly attached to that blood as the only organically possible access to the very spirit of every offspring of Adam. And all of his progeny who would share that similar animal blood in faith looking forward to the Redeemer would have their names written in His Book of Life.

And along the way, others have seen glimpses of the end of the path.

When the Lord brought Israel out of Egypt, the final blow that moved the Pharaoh to let Israel go was the loss of every firstborn male, unless protected by the animal blood smeared on the doorpost. And in the process, we know the whole land of Egypt was covered in a thick, palpable, supernatural darkness for three days, the same kind of darkness evident at the crucifixion, and the same time Jesus' body would lie in the tomb.

And later, Abraham saw it from another vantage point as the blood covenant was furthered through him.

> *And behold the word of the LORD came*
> *to him saying, "This one [Ishmael] shall*
> *not be your heir, but one who will come*

from your own body shall be your heir."
Then He brought him outside and said,
"Look now toward heaven, and count the
stars if you able to number them." And
He said to him, "So shall your descen-
dants be."
And he believed the LORD, and He
accounted it to him for righteousness.
Then He said to him, "I am the LORD, who
brought you out of Ur of the Chaldeans,
to give you this land to inherit it."
And he said, "Lord GOD, how shall I
know that I will inherit it?"
So He said to him, "Bring Me a three-
year-old heifer, a three-year-old female
goat, a three-year-old ram, a turtledove,
and a young pigeon."
Then he brought all these to Him and
cut them in two, down the middle, and
placed each piece opposite the other;
but he did not cut the birds in two. And
when the vultures came down on the
carcasses, Abram drove them away.
Now when the sun was going down, a
deep sleep fell upon Abram; and behold,
horror and great darkness fell upon
him.....And it came to pass, when the sun

*went down and it was dark, that behold,
there appeared a smoking oven and a
burning torch that passed between those
pieces.*   Genesis 15:4-12, 17

Plainly, Abraham was physically immobilized
and in a spiritually sensitized state via the Holy
Spirit. (A lexicon notes that the Hebrew term translated as a 'horror and great darkness' are also later
used to describe God's appearance on Mt Sinai.)
And it takes two for a covenant. While he was thus
in the Spirit, a smoking furnace (God the Father)
and a burning lamp (Jesus; think of the temple
menorah later) walked between the halves of the
carcasses to bind the covenant, Jesus on behalf of
Abraham and his future offspring.

If God abandoned Jesus on the cross, then He
is a covenant-breaker!

Abraham experienced the same supernatural
darkness others, later, would at Calvary, only from
a different perspective. And he could see the work
of God that went with it, as Jesus told the religious
detractors of his day. *"Your father Abraham rejoiced
to see My day, and saw it and was glad"* (John 8:56).

And there is yet that final confrontation
approaching soon when all the forces of darkness,

natural and supernatural, gather for their last-ditch confrontation with the Lord:

> *A day of darkness and gloominess, a day of clouds and thick darkness, like the morning clouds spread over the mountains. A people come, great and strong, the like of whom has never been; Nor will ever be any such after them, even for many successive generations.*
>
> Joel 2:2

The Day of the Lord is the reference, and the resurrection of dead believers and removal to heaven, along with living believers, before the amazed eyes of a watching world. There is no doubt the Rapture is imminent. When even Hollywood is making a somewhat realistic movie of it, it has to be near!

Whatever your end-time timing conviction is—Pre, Mid or Post Tribulation—(the reader might have already concluded that the author is unabashedly Pre) the issue of importance is the race.

Is the Church running crippled or not? And if so, what needs to change?

While the bottom line message of the gospel presented to the world is included, so much of the hidden workings of salvation has been lost and explained away that it sometimes amazes me that the message has succeeded as much as it has; it is only because there is a supernatural God working behind it.

The default story line of the accepted Christian message is that a righteous and Holy God demands blood for a universal punishment for any and every sin, small or large, and He got it by killing His own Son. Think of Jonathan Edwards' 1741 sermon, "Sinners in the Hands of an Angry God" delivered during the height of the Great Awakening in America. That's what it took then to awaken some in sleeping churches, but that is not the complete story, as we have seen here.

That is a picture that, in concentrated doses, presents God as a vengeful stickler for absolute justice at any price; who is the judge, jury and executioner, the author of death; ready to hand it out for anyone who doesn't measure up to His standard of behavior.

And one of the unintended fruits of that presentation is numbers of people who want nothing to do with Christianity because that message condemns them and presents them with a list of things they can't do (dress, appearance, food, entertainment, etc.) if they want God's acceptance, when they are already accepted in Christ Jesus! Untold numbers reject the message they did not hear when Christians look down on them and offer no help. All of India was lost to a move of God when Mahatma Gandhi, looking for the way to God, saw no Christ-likeness in the Christians he met, and seeing only a model for moral behavior, concluded Christianity gave him nothing he didn't already have in his Hindu religion.

The challenge is, again, to the Church, believers. We are the ones commissioned with the task to take the fellowship of the mystery not only to the world, but exhibit it to the unseen hosts in the supernatural realm (see Ephesians 3:9). And not only to the world, but to God's own people, the Jews:

> *For I do not desire, brethren, that you should be ignorant of this mystery, lest you should be wise in you own opinion, that blindness in part has happened to Israel until the fullness of the Gentiles has come in. And so all Israel will be saved, as it is written:*
>
> *"The Deliverer will come out of Zion, And He will turn away ungodliness from Jacob; For this is My covenant with them, When I take away their sins."*
>
> *Concerning the gospel they are enemies for your sake, but concerning the*

election they are beloved for the sake of the fathers. For the gifts and the calling of God are irrevocable.   Romans 11:25-29

How many Jews might have recognized their Messiah had the Church known the true story, bypassing all the anti-Semitic behavior? That was to be expected from the world, but from God's people? By any reasonable test, the Church as a whole has fallen way short in its race, and too much of the Lord's harvest has been lost.

And the major factor is that, as we have seen here, the gospel message has never quite graduated from the message for the Jewish audience to the covenant that really was the original from Adam—the fellowship of the mystery, which from the beginning of the ages has been hidden in God who created all things through Jesus Christ.

The gospel is a conception, your conception if you will or have turned to Jesus.

Chapter Twelve

Pivotal History

Much of this book likely strikes the reader as distinctly different from anything ever heard in church before; perhaps all of it does! As a concluding vehicle to help the reader identify the place and importance of the message, six pivotal points in our history, both secular and religious, are briefly summarized (some recaps of the book) to show the historical flow that makes this message, as I believe, the last revelation of the Church Age.

1. Satan Starts War

If there were a newspaper in heaven, that could have been the headline on the day when the pride of Satan (then named Lucifer) got the better of him. Revelation 12:7-9 is the summary:

*And war broke out in heaven: Michael
and his angels fought with the dragon;
and the dragon and his angels fought,
but they did not prevail, nor was a place
found for them in heaven any longer.
So the great dragon was cast out, the
serpent of old, called the Devil and
Satan, who deceives the whole world;
he was cast to the earth, and his angels
were cast out with him.*

2. War Arrives on Earth; Earth Taken Prisoner; God Tells the End from the Beginning

And those were the headlines for earth on that day in the garden of Eden. When Satan came to the garden, it was with one objective: to become the god of this world. Adam was the created god of this world, given the commission from God, the creator and owner (see Genesis 1:28). When Adam yielded to Satan's deception, he yielded his dominion over the earth to Satan. Adam's body being made from the earth, he too became the prisoner of Satan, and all his family tree fell subject to the sickness and slavery of death that Satan spread with his deception (see Romans 5:12). The war had become a war with *pneumo* (spirit)-biogenetic proportions, played out in the spirit dimension *and* the material realm of biology, passed genetically to an entire race.

God told Satan what he should expect as the end of his rebellion—*"And I will put enmity between you and the woman, and between your seed and her Seed; He shall bruise your head, and you shall bruise His heel"* (Genesis 3:15).

The war's outcome would be settled by each side's champion. God put in place a blood sacrifice that would lead to His champion: the Seed of the woman.

3. Radical Measures; Noah's Flood

Satan knew enough of God to know that God meant what He said. That called for radical tactics:

> *Now it came to pass, when men began to multiply on the earth, and daughters were born to them, that the sons of God (angels) saw the daughters of men, that they were beautiful; and they took wives for themselves of all whom they chose....*
>
> *There were giants on the earth in those days, and also afterward, when the*

> *sons of God came in to the daughters*
> *of men and they bore children to them.*
> *Those were the mighty men of old, men*
> *of renown.*   Genesis 6:1-2, 4

This radical tactic was calculated to succeed on three fronts. First, the giant offspring naturally became worshiped as gods (since they were the products of angels). This, of course, diverted worship from God, putting worshippers squarely in the rebellious camp. Second, the angelic leaders instituted imitation blood sacrifices, causing participants to lose hold of the one long-term safety element they otherwise had available. And third, their program of corrupting the human genome was calculated to leave no inherited genetic thread for the Seed of the woman to trace without genetic modification, cutting the blood lifeline short. Along with that, imitating the blood sacrifices with practices that demanded killing their firstborn males would hopefully kill anyone who could be the Seed of the woman, a precursor to Herod's similar attempt to kill the Messiah when He would later be born (see Matthew 2:16).

Those radical tactics had such success that God was moved to destroy all life on earth (see Genesis

6:7), except eight people—one family, who had remained above the practices Satan had introduced.

> *But Noah found grace in the eyes of*
> *the Lord. This is the genealogy of Noah.*
> *Noah was a just man, perfect in his gen-*
> *erations. Noah walked with God."*
>
> Genesis 6:8-9

In spite of that worldwide deluge, Genesis 6:4 tells us that not only did Satan's angels attempt that genetic corruption of the human race before the flood, but also again after the flood. Hearing God's promise to never again bring such a flood, they were emboldened to try a second time.

4. Resolution: Christ and the Cross

An intact thread of bloodline from Adam to Joseph and Mary transmitted through Joseph the right to reclaim world control, and through Mary, the genetic purity as the prophesied Seed of the woman. And having arrived as promised, Jesus became the one who represented the fullness of all the Godhead in material flesh—flesh conceived, and anointed without measure by the Holy Spirit. His life and ministry were without reproach—Satan had nothing in Him (see John 14:30). And the final work of His ministry—His death and resurrection—allowed the Holy Spirit, via intercession, circumcision, and baptism, to follow the unbroken blood path back 4000 years to Adam, and then forward to all Adam's offspring for resurrection (with new bodies). Those who kept faith in God's original blood covenant would see a resurrection to be with the Lord forever; those who disdained it to a resurrection forever excluded from His presence.

And Satan? With Jesus' resurrection, and that of the Old Testament righteous saints, he was openly shown to have lost his power to hold men captive (see Ephesians 4:8). The moment he lost it is the subject of several religious opinions, but I see the moment Satan's delegated representative, the Roman soldier, put a crown on Jesus' head, it was as good as all over—he lost it the same way he gained it from Adam, by a free will decision.

5. The Dark Ages

Not one to willingly let go of power, the Bible relates that Satan immediately stirred up a fury of persecution against God's people, both Jews and Christians. When persecution didn't wipe out the fledgling Christian movement, a three-pronged plan was next.

Undestroyed by persecution, Christianity was granted secular recognition in 313 by Emperors Constantine (ruling the Western Roman Empire) and Licinius (ruling the Eastern) in the Concordat of Milan. That recognition later turned to state control of the organized church and the loss of much biblical and spiritual awareness during the Middle Ages, also known as the Dark Ages.

In another quarter, Satan raised up an imitation religion as Mohamed and his followers started to overrun much of the Middle East with Islam, ultimately reaching west into Europe as far as France, east into India and north into the Balkan countries.

When the Muslims captured Alexandria, Egypt, and reportedly burned the world-famous library there, Europe's one source of paper was cut off; books became scarce and European Catholic churches would chain the Bible to the pulpit, claiming it was too holy to let the common people read it.

Co-opt control, eliminate by the sword, remove the source of knowledge—Satan's devices of the Dark Ages. Various reformation movements, described together as the Protestant Reformation, started in efforts to bring the Bible to public availability and return Christian belief and practice to biblical standards.

We might read into God's instructions to Daniel that God was expecting we would need an infusion of revelation in our times to counter Satan's devices, *"But you, Daniel, shut up the words, and seal the book, until the time of the end; many shall run to and fro, and knowledge shall increase"* (Daniel 12:4).

6. Our Day: Reprise Noah

Those collective events brought us to today. Today we are in what the Bible calls the Last Days; Jesus told His disciples that this time would climax with the Resurrection on the last day (see John 6:39-40). Amid much supportive expectation in some religious quarters (both Christian and Muslim), doubt or unconcern in perhaps much of the Christian church, and denial and unconcern in the world at large, there is only one way to know of a certainty— what does the Bible say? What does God say?

The twenty-fourth chapter of Matthew contains Jesus's answer as He responds to His disciples' questions, *"Tell us, when will these things be* (the destruction of the temple He had just predicted in verse 2)*? And what will be the sign of Your coming, and of the end of the age?"* The details He gives following those questions have been objects of scrutiny to this day: *"wars and rumors of wars"* (v. 6) and *"famines, pestilences, and earthquakes in various places"* (v. 7) are the most widely speculated signs. But the wars and rumors of wars, Jesus said to be not troubled over, *"for all these things must come to pass, but the end is not yet."*

We've seen a constant stream of wars with attendant famines and pestilences from then until now. And yes, we have seen a noticeable increase in numbers of earthquakes, but the hallmark purpose for what may appear to be delay, He says, is that *"this gospel of the kingdom will be preached in all the world as a witness to all nations, and then the end will come"* (v. 14).

Today, the gospel has been preached around the world, and is available over the Internet 24 hours a day, but we might still be hard pressed to find a generally acknowledged starting point for the End Times just on the strength of that. But we need not, because Jesus continued, giving us exactly the event that should cause us to begin our expectation:

> *Now learn this parable from the fig tree: When its branch has already become tender and puts forth leaves, you know that summer is near. So you also, when you see all these things, know that it is near—at the doors! Assuredly, I say to*

you, this generation (that sees all these things happening) *will by no means pass away till all these things take place.*"   Matthew 24: 33-34

The fig tree, in the scriptures, is representative of Israel. For 1900 years, none of what Jesus described as the end times applied, because Israel had no national existence after Rome destroyed Jerusalem and the Temple in 70AD, until 1947, when in a single day, it regained national existence by action of the United Nations. So November 29, 1947 (or May 14, 1948 if you start from its declaration of statehood) set the prophetic clock ticking toward the end. The psalmist wrote in Psalms 90:10, *"The days of our lives are seventy years. . ."* Coupled to a personalized Israel, 70 years brings us to the year 2017—not that far off.

There are a number of other prophetic developments that point to the time frame from September of 2015 (the timing of blood moons and solar eclipses with the festivals of the Jewish calendar) to 2017, along with the world political and economic conditions.

Two groups have a positive stake in that prophetic clock: Jews and Christians. Without lengthy exhaustive presentation of scripture, but enough to clearly identify the reasons for today's concern, here are the key applications for each.

For Jews, all revolves around Daniel's Old Testament prophecy of seventy weeks (sevens) of years pronounced against Israel (Daniel 9:24-27). After sixty-nine weeks, the Messiah would be killed. The final week (seven years) would see the person we know as the antichrist beginning the period confirming a peace treaty, and break it midway through the period. The final seven-year period ends with world-wide war, chaos and destruction, culminating in Jesus' return to save Jewish Israel, destroy the armies of the antichrist, and throw Satan into prison for a thousand years.

Obviously the first sixty-nine weeks of years and the final week (seven years) have been separated by what Christians call the Church Age for the purpose of spreading the gospel to the whole world. Christians too are motivated to track that final seven years. That final seven years is part of a determined period of judgment on Israel and the world. Paul writes that believers (Christians) are not appointed to wrath, but to salvation (see 1 Thessalonians 5:9.) He also wrote to the early Thessalonian church not to be shaken by the persecution of the day, thinking they had missed the Resurrection and Rapture. He writes,

Now brethren, concerning the coming of our Lord Jesus Christ and our gathering together to Him, we ask you, not to be soon shaken in mind or troubled, either by spirit or by word or by letter, as if from us, as though the day of Christ had come. Let no one deceive you by any means; for that Day will not come unless the falling away (Greek apostasia, meaning "departure"; other translation usage includes "departure from a belief") comes first, and the man of sin is revealed, the son of perdition, who opposes and exalts himself above all that is called God or that is worshipped, so that he sits as God in the temple of God, showing himself that he is God." 2 Thessalonians 2:1-4

Pre-, Mid-, or Post-

There are three camps of Christian belief about the point in time when Christians as the figurative Bride of Christ are resurrected and removed from earth (the Rapture) to meet Jesus in the clouds to go to heaven for the wedding supper—before (pre-tribulation), middle (mid-tribulation) and after (post-tribulation.)

Paul was the one person who was given the revelation of believers' resurrection and the timing with respect to the final seven-year period of judgment. It happens before the identity of the antichrist is revealed, and his identity is revealed at the beginning of the seven years when he confirms a peace treaty. With all due respect to other opinions, that's pretty clear—before.

No matter which we believe, our opinion won't change the times that God has fixed. The point for us here is what Jesus went on to say to His disciples in Matthew, Chapter 24 (echoed also in Luke 17:26) concerning the day He would return to rescue Israel:

> *But of that day and hour no one knows, not even the angels of heaven, but My Father only.* (Keep in mind here that He was speaking to Jewish disciples who yet had no clue about the 1900-year church age we have experienced.) ***But as the days of Noah were, so also will the coming of the Son of Man be.*** *For as in the days before the flood, they were eating and drinking, marrying and giving in marriage, until the*

*day that Noah entered the ark, and did
not know until the flood came and took
them all away, so also will the coming
of the Son of Man be.*   Vv.36-39

Most people who read these verses focus on two concepts presented in it. One is the unknown timing (vv. 36, 39), the second is a derived idea of the general evilness of society, assuming that was the state of society in Noah's day that made God draw the line. There is some light that other scriptures shed on these two conclusions that should really make believers reconsider such views.

The first concerns the unknown timing. For believers, that relates to the timing of the Rapture. Noah's ark is a precursor type of the safety believers have in Christ. Genesis 7:4 tells us that in Noah's case, God told him exactly when to expect the rain; God gave him a seven-day warning before the destruction began. Appreciators of God's meticulous sense of order and detail could see a parallel there between the seven days of Noah's flood and the approaching seven years of destruction our day faces. As part of that unknown timing, consider who were the ones that had no knowledge of the timing (or perhaps even of the impending event)—those who were about to be destroyed, the world society.

That presents another interesting similarity to those today who generally dismiss the imminence of Jesus' return for His bride by saying that we can't know timing; perhaps we can, but haven't been paying attention. Jesus' parable of the ten virgins (Matthew 25:1-13), five of whom missed the wedding, left a clear challenge to those not paying attention!

The second area of concern, I believe the most challenging, is recognizing the condition that caused a near wipeout of the entire human race, and will again shortly. Jesus, continuing to speak to His disciples:

> *For there will be great tribulation, such as has not been since the beginning of the world until this time, no, nor ever shall be. And unless those days were shortened, no flesh would be saved; but for the elect's sake those days will be shortened.... For false christs and false prophets will rise and show great signs and wonders to deceive, if possible, even the elect.*
>
> Matthew 24:21-22, 24

We are in a war, and the stakes are nothing less than the earth and its entire population; as Satan makes his last stand, he does not care how much collateral damage occurs.

Details of this damage are left to the book of Revelation, among them a fourth of earth's population killed by violence, starvation and the beasts of the earth (see Revelation 6:8), massive earthquakes, 100 pound hailstones, hoards of demonic entities released (see Revelation 5:1-11), and an army of two hundred million loosed to kill a third of mankind (see Revelation 9:15) to cite just several.

We could go on at length just looking at the extent of the carnage, but as even a surface inquiry shows, and the Bible clearly predicts, the general world population senses something coming, but remains largely unconcerned.

The more pressing concern is that too many in the ranks of Christianity are no more concerned than the world and are equally unprepared for what is coming on the earth. This condition exists, to a great extent I believe, because of the inaccuracy of the historical gospel message and the related omission or denial of the reason for both Noah's flood and the end that is now almost upon us.

The reason for both Noah's flood and the things coming on the earth in our day, Jesus plainly told the disciples. What happened in Noah's day? *"There were giants on the earth in those days, and also afterward, when the sons of God came in to the daughters of men, and they bore children to them"* (Genesis 6:4).

This describes a massive, deliberate attempt to make permanent the Satanic control over the earth and its inhabitants. It wasn't an effort from another material planet; it was an invasion from another dimension.

And the start traces to God's pronouncement after Adam's unfortunate garden choice, *"And I will put enmity between you* (Satan) *and the woman, and between your seed and her Seed* (Jesus); *He shall bruise your head, and you shall bruise his heel"* (Genesis 3:15). We are experiencing the closing scenes of this 'seed' war.

The Seed War

God produced His Seed (Jesus) who dethroned Satan. In the approaching final scenes of this age, the Bible describes Satan using the same tactic— flesh incarnation—as a platform for deceptive supernatural miracles.

To add to the cast of characters, God's description of the scenes the world is presently facing describes additional intrusions from the other dimension. In the second chapter of Daniel, picturing the succession of kingdoms that will (and have) come to power as parts of the statue that Babylonian king Nebuchadnezzar saw in a dream, the last kingdom is pictured as the ten toes of the statue. Remember that behind every political power we see physically, there is an angelic person ruling it from the other dimension. God describes the ten 'toes' to Daniel (which, in the seventh chapter of Daniel are described as giving their power to another, the 'little horn' likely representing Satan's incarnate seed), *"As you saw iron mixed with ceramic clay, **they will mingle with the seed of men**; but they will not adhere to one another, just as iron does not mix with clay"* (Daniel 2:43).

Here, the same language is used which, we know from history, describes biogenetic results. The point is that what we can see physically happening in the world is a result of a planned, hostile incursion from another dimension. And it is reflected across several areas—genetics, biology, science, politics, economics and religion to name several, and in several mediums.

The resolution of the human condition is the resolution of this war's hostile pneumo-biogenetic attack. It is absolutely and categorically impossible to fully and accurately understand the reality and operation of the salvation mystery without fully embracing this reality. Does that make me a conspiracy believer?

Absolutely! As my grandfather was fond of pointing out, it isn't paranoia if someone really is out to get you.

That is a radically different historical and religious view than commonly believed. It has taken some time and a lot of reading others' research to see the real picture myself. And here I simply must request the reader's cooperation. To thoroughly present all evidence across the areas of Satanic activity would take a number of volumes, mostly recounting others' research. I endeavor to present enough to you to give a large-scope picture, but in the final analysis, if you would have the foundation to deal with what is controlling the world, I must do as Jesus did and trust that you have ears to hear. (In addition, there are helpful links on my website: www.SeeTheMystery.org.)

Given that the key to this war is the biogenetic bloodline trace to Adam—preserving it for God to regain control, or blocking and replacing it for Satan to retain control—a central effort of Satan centers on what has come to be described as transhumanism.

The online Oxford dictionary defines transhumanism as: "The belief or theory that the human race can evolve beyond its current physical and mental limitations, especially by means of science and technology."

Wikipedia defines transhumanism as: "an ideology and movement which seeks to develop and make available technologies that eliminate aging and greatly enhance human intellectual, physical, and psychological capacities, in order to achieve a post-human future." Wikipedia may not be a professionally edited dictionary, but by the fact of its public-supplied creation and contribution, it expresses the general public's understanding and expectation. There is a lot in there that is enticing until a person gets to the end. Who wouldn't like to see science overcome sickness and aging? Living forever is the universal human challenge and desire. From Ponce De Leon's search for the fabled fountain of youth to science's current efforts to produce 100+ year life extensions as a common thing, always just beyond the horizon is that post-human future. The very term 'post-human' as the goal ought to raise a real red flag in anyone's mind. If the goal is to be something other than human, what is the product going to be? And who is going to provide it? By either of the above definitions, it is without God's input.

We are told what the result was for the first and second post-human occasions—giants; frightening beings of intimidating size (variously described as 10 to 25+ feet tall) with 6 fingers on each hand and 6 toes on each foot. Recent excavations and testing have yielded remains and genetic tests showing results that are distinctly different from the human genome. In short the post-human goal is exactly what lured Adam and Eve—that you might be as God.

Looking back through history, this always was the end of tyrant rulers—Roman emperors who demanded worship as gods are only one example among many. Occult-obsessed Adolf Hitler sought the perfection of a new Aryan race. More recent false religious organizations also have this at the heart. If you research early published Mormon literature, you find the assertion that Jesus is just a man who was somehow able to climb to a higher state of development, as followers should be able to do. This is the end goal of the son of perdition we anticipate as the antichrist, *"who opposes and exalts himself above all that is called God or that is worshiped, so that he sits as God in the temple of God, showing himself that he is God"* (2 Thessalonians 2:4).

The New Age Movement

The New Age Movement refers to the same general organized purpose. Built on earlier organizations like the Theosophical Society (organized by Helena Blavatsky in 1875), which focused on occultism, New Age Movement activity focuses on Eastern and pagan religions, mother-earth worship and channeling spirits from another dimension. The Bible identifies those channeled spirits as demonic entities.

Much of what is presented for our entertainment consumption (films, television, music) pushes the same story line and similar occult themes. The common storyline is that there is no God, just an advanced race out in space somewhere that seeded our planet with the beginning of our human race, and who will return soon to save us from ecological self-destruction and help us ascend to a next stage in spiritual development. (*Stargate* and *Prometheus* are just a couple of such movies, while television has shown such shows as *Falling Skies* and *Resurrection*, which is a blatant mimicking of the resurrection Christian believers anticipate.)

Both movies and television mediums also supply products with human-alien mixtures (The movie *Splice* comes to mind, and the present network show *Marvel's Agents of S.H.I.E.L.D.* gives us two savior figures that are changed by alien blood.) The TV show *V*, of several seasons ago, gave us reptilian invaders skinned to look like us. A previous season of the cable SyFy channel aired the show *Dominion*, wherein God supposedly has mysteriously disappeared, and in His absence the earth is overrun by a faction of angels who possess and mate with humans—again, the invasion of another dimension for a genetic purpose. Add all the occult and paranormal shows, and society is awash in occult influences.

UFOs

The other area that I strongly urge the reader to research is the subject of UFOs. Just don't view the speculation of the History Channel's offerings (*Ancient Aliens* and *UFO Chronicles*) as the real explanation; they both ignore the real source—Satanic invasion from the spirit dimension.

As you become familiar with the documented intrusions from what we label UFOs, there are a couple of key realities that apply to our purpose here.

One is the frequency of activity. Graphed against time, reported activity has taken exponential increases at two times in recent history, once in 1897 when the World Zionist Congress, under the leadership of Theodor Herzl, adopted the purpose of creation of a Jewish state in Palestine; and again in 1947 when Israel become a national entity. The correlation with scriptural end-time events is arresting.

The second is to clearly apprehend the underlying purpose. Accounts of UFO abductions all seem to have the same elements indicating a genetic program aimed at producing beings indistinguishable from us.

Technology, too, is racing to this same target. One UK (British) laboratory announced recently that they have created 155 human-animal hybrids. As this book goes to print, the author received a notice of one company's new genetic treatment product announcing that, with a series of four injections, a subject's human DNA will be spliced and changed with the addition of animal genetic material to make the person live functionally forever – the 'immortality gene'.

And this fits exactly with what scripture says to expect. Satan had two earlier tries at genetic manipulation. Giants were pretty easy to spot . For his approaching final attempt, he's had 2000 years of preparation to make the product visually indistinguishable from us, but capable of supernatural miracles that will have people convinced that maybe that New Age stuff wasn't just nonsense. He doesn't want the product to visually stand out; this time he wants it to blend in until the big reveal! And when it's time for the big reveal, New Age writings anticipate the resurrection and removal of believers in the clouds, with a story line that people who aren't spiritually ready for the next jump in human development will have been removed from the earth to let the final step take place for those remaining behind on earth.

It seems to me a distinct possibility that people who are only casual Christians because of the powerlessness of an inaccurate legal crime-and-punishment view may be highly at risk for a massive deception that will seem to have no trouble exhibiting amazing powers.

Chapter Thirteen

Conclusion

It has been observed that people tend to embrace the fellowship of caring people before they commit to a belief system. I've heard it put thus, "People don't care about how much you know until they know how much you care." And that is the experience that cults commonly use to draw the down-and-out.

This same concern for others is the expected trait that should make every Christian an open and compelling invitation to Christ. Paul likens believers to epistles read by all men (see 2 Corinthians 3:2.) But while personal fellowship with others brings people to church, it is the accuracy and completeness of the gospel message people hear that determine the quality of the decision they can make for Jesus.

With that conviction, I include my own personal thoughts as both summary and conclusions concerning the contents of this book.

Though it seems a project of huge scope, the Christian message must be replaced with a clear, accurate picture; and quickly. Here is a summary of the reasons why:

- The accepted gospel message is dangerously inaccurate, occurring by a combination of stealth error introduced by the enemy (Satan), ignorant entertainment of those errors by the Church, and insufficient revelation in the church, sometimes willingly, sometimes not. Observing how denominations seem to have formed over points of contention that could have been resolved by subsequent revelatory understanding, I can only think that the Church would be much less fractured if all shared the same full perspective of the gospel as a conception.

  From experience I know that clear and complete understanding closes some doors to cult activity. One of my childhood friends is still staunchly committed to a well-known cult because a denominational minister couldn't explain the fundamentals of the Christian faith to him after friendly cult members came to his door during a time when he was seeking to understand faith.

- The basis for salvation is not the crime-and-punishment model religious discussions and messages have presented.
- The basis for salvation is personal conception and regeneration in the spirit realm by the Holy Spirit.
- Defined as written or verbal agreements and promises, we are familiar with written Old Testament and New Testament, and within the Old Testament, successive sub-covenants—the Abrahamic Covenant and the Davidic Covenant. Seen as a medium, we know the blood of animals as a covering typified the Old Testament from Adam on, and the Blood of Christ is the medium of the New Testament, which replaced the old. But taken as the thing that vitally connects us to God, the reality is this: Scripture shows us unmistakably that, from God's perspective, there has been only one underlying Covenant, one blood covenant that dated from Adam; it was a covenant between the Father and the Son. We just happened to be the beneficiaries.
- The Bible is a revelatory book from beginning to end. Even the introduction of the Old Testament Law through Moses can be seen as a revelation of the forces that had been

in effect for 3,600 years, but un-published until Israel's disobedience made it necessary. Applying Jesus' post-resurrection announcement of the Great Commission and believers' authority can be seen with the same perspective. When Jesus announced the Great Commission in Matthew 28:18 and19, saying, *"All authority has been given to Me in heaven and on earth. Go therefore. . ."* we read it as delegating His mission. The only reason for the *"therefore"* is that Jesus had, by that time, all authority. An equally accurate understanding can see that commission as a command couched in revelation. Any commission or authority resident in Jesus was, after His resurrection, shared by His body the Church simply by virtue of the fact that He made believers one with Himself. Mark's account of the Great Commission couples the two perhaps more clearly as revelation:

And He said to them, "Go into all the world and preach the gospel to every creature. He who believes and is baptized will be saved; but he who does not believe will be condemned. And these signs will follow those who believe: In

My name they will cast out demons; they will speak with new tongues; they will take up serpents; and if they drink anything deadly, it will by no means hurt them; they will lay hands on the sick, and they will recover." Mark 16:15-17

This was not so much a statement delegating power for miracles as a revelatory statement of what the new norm should be.

- Scripture cautions believers against being sensual. This refers, not to being engaged in things relating to sex, but judging things by what appears to the physical senses. The unseen supernatural realm is much more extensive than the physical material world, and can only be apprehended by revelation.
- Not only is the Bible a revelatory book, it is a book of progressive revelation. As time has progressed, God has supplied more and more understanding of His salvation operation. When unfolding world events now show us what prophecy was really describing, we can better appreciate why Daniel was told that understanding some of what he saw should be sealed up until the time of the end (see Daniel 12:4). And now that we are so close

to the return of the Lord, it is absolutely important to have the entire picture accurately understood.

- Not realizing the reality of the one underlying covenant, general practice has come to disregard the first 3,600 years of our history and let the world rewrite God out of it. Jewish culture tends to see themselves as the covenant people. During some periods in the past, the Church, thinking Jews have been bypassed, believed Christians are now the sole covenant people, neither group seeing the complete picture. Recent thought changes within the Church have come to recognize the common Jewish roots, but without seeing the beginning-to-end scope, almost have the tone of trying to revert Christian practice to the Jewish model.

- The legality gospel message, built on Old Testament Law, imposes limits. Seeing Christianity as adopted or grafted into the Jewish experience (or perhaps the justified-only product of that experience) makes the 400 years of the Mosaic Law become its only history.

- If there is no clear organic reality in the Christian message, whether to the Jew or to the Christian, then Christianity can become more of a cultural thing of choice, much as Judaism is to some Jews. And that is a dangerous position, because it excludes a relationship with God as a personal experience.

- The legal punishment dialogue presents an inaccurate picture of God as the author of death, the punisher of every imperfection. Thus, it reinforces the erroneous belief that anything bad that happens is God punishing you for something. Who would want to run to a God who loads on all kinds of misfortune?

- While impressive that the Church has evangelized the world, it is still done with a legality dialogue that symbolizes away a real, born-again conception. (That's why, after a salvation decision, people require so much foundational teaching to get it to work for them in the real world.) People then only know they are legally forgiven of punishment for works committed to that moment, not that they are organically conceived by God, born of the Spirit. Even with continued reinforcement of the once-punished-for-all-offences-forever picture, the nagging wonder about today's shortcomings still limits many believers. People can only live up to what they know of themselves.

- The believer is a transformed, new species of creature, a child of the Living God by conception, not just the same old sinner forgiven. (If the message tells them they are the same old person, just legally forgiven, then they will likely keep living the same way, never rising to the life of a child of the Living God.) Not that forgiveness isn't part of the picture. Jesus had some strong direct things to say about its necessity. It is the innately accompanying result of the born-again experience, not the reverse. Without launching into an in-depth study here, let's just point out that some word studies easily show that the effect of forgiveness in scripture is described as removing the attached power of some spirit-realm entity (let's say some sickness caused by a demonic spirit, who perhaps gained a hold because of something the person did.) When Jesus forgave sins, the result was healing, but not being born again. Even in the New Testament, believers are invested with the authority to loose and retain sins, reaching even into the operations of heaven (see Matthew 16:19,

18:18), but the only test of born again is to recognize and accept Jesus.

- In a message built on legal vicarious punishment, with 'born again' being explained as symbolic, in the mind of God, accounted, imputed or positional, the inclination sooner or later takes on the flavor of salvation by works. When that happens, what is heard, granted not by intent, can be a set of rules that repel people. A recent survey showed that the reason the present generation of 18-33 year olds don't come to church is that they are bored and repelled by rules. (If they think all church is boring, wait until they get in a Holy Ghost meeting with signs, wonders and miracles going on!) If the reality is only symbolic, the works are the only thing left that touches real life. The gift of salvation and the reward of our works become too-easily merged to the point that churchgoers never hear the invitation that would save them.

- Rationality is another challenge. The assertion of the crime-and-punishment-gospel is that vicarious punishment causes a born-again experience. Rational thought knows that the one isn't a rational cause-and-effect result of the other; there has to be more to the story. As noted in the previous point, symbolism, or legal accounting, or 'in the mind of God' become the explanations—all of them irrational. In that dialogue, faith becomes defined as irrational as the norm—it's not expected to make sense. And irrational faith tends to produce either passive, do-nothing religion or extremes of action to justify itself. That need to define faith as irrational has opened the door to all manner of irrational corruptions, and made it unappealing to rational people. (e.g. The belief that you have to handle venomous snakes to prove faith comes to mind.) More than that, to be taken literally, strong Christian faith becomes crazy by definition, and who wants to be labeled as crazy? By not giving a complete picture, the doors are left open to conjecture and imagination from every quarter.

- The very irrationality of the conventional born-again explanation also opens doors for the seemingly rational error of Universalism. (If everything depends on punishment, and God did it universally and acceptably for everyone, then it becomes believable that all will be saved, no matter what.)

- Presented with the gospel as it has been with the inconsistencies, a believer commonly is confronted with a choice of either doing without the benefits that are his (like healing, or manifestations of the Spirit) since common religious thought has explained them away, or after much additional instruction, feel like he has to somehow work them into manifestation (which can be too close to thinking of the subject in a works perspective.) Additional instruction does yield results. But my point is that if people know the whole picture from the outset, all these elements never have to suffer the question, "Is this included in salvation?" People can know it and be convinced of it from the very start. Then people are more in the position of just letting the Word work instead of feeling like they have to make it work (for a manifestation).

- Many believers who are aware of Christ's imminent return are expecting a great revival, bigger that anything to date, before His return for the Church. I earnestly hope we experience that. But studying past revivals, one thing is clear: revival never just happens. Someone starts it. Someone actively desires it. Someone presses for it. Prayer is always involved. But my question is this: If we are expecting an experience like never before, and only the same elements are in play (prayer, etc.), then how can we rationally expect anything different from the past. If the message has been limited, then perhaps that is the one place we need to start.

- The other troubling part of that assumption is that God can't proceed with the program unless such a big revival happens. Here, I can only relate the experience of another more experienced than myself. I studied under a minister who was one of the most notable of our day. He was a prophet, not self-proclaimed like most self-labelers, but commissioned from the hand of Jesus directly, with all the manifestations of the Spirit active in his ministry, who was, by Jesus' expressed announcement to this minister's parents, the one who would occupy the John the Baptist role for His return. There were times when he said that the Holy Spirit wanted to do a move in the Church, but could not until people readied themselves; and if they didn't, the move of the Holy Spirit would be lost. Just because God wants a great move is no guarantee it will happen.

- Part of the race, individually and collectively, is winning others. (Perhaps the largest part of the race; that is, after all, the only commission of the Great Commission.) If we aren't doing that, there will be some highly ashamed people when the crowns are passed out. The only way it works is for the gospel to be preached, God working to confirm His Word with signs following. If the Word isn't being preached accurately, how should we expect Him to confirm it? As we have seen, the historical message has been built on an assumed perspective. If we have seen world-changing results with a limited-accuracy message, think what could be done with the fully accurate message!

- And finally, Jesus said four conditions would be necessary before the end comes. First, Israel would be re-gathered to their land—accomplished. Second, the times would be as the days of Noah (Luke 17:26)—in motion. Third, it would be as the days of Sodom and Gomorrah (Luke 17:28,29)—homosexuality proclaimed as the law of the land by our recent Supreme Court's deliberations. And fourth, that the gospel should be preached in all the world (Mark 16:15)—we've heard a legal-oriented Jewish experience presentation, but from the time Paul penned his epistles, we haven't, until now, had a picture of the complete workings of the real supernatural gospel available.

I am praying you, the reader, will finish your race with joy, and hear that ultimately satisfying "Well done" when you stand before the Master.

Time is short and the finish line is in sight!

And What Will You Do?

———•>•◦•<•———

You may have heard little or much about God and Christianity in your life. You may have attended or even grown up in church and never come to the point of committing to a decision. Perhaps the message never made sense or seemed compelling. The decision that will change you, put you in God's family and give you a new future is the recognition and acceptance of Jesus Christ as your God and Savior.

Having now heard the gospel, will you make that decision? If so, simply voice it to Him. If you don't know quite what to say, here is a simple prayer you can use:

Jesus, I recognize You as God, the One who reclaimed me from Satan's death and offered me Your life and Spirit to make me a child of the Living God.

I willingly and joyfully accept.
Today I start my new supernatural life
with and in You.
Amen.

CPSIA information can be obtained
at www.ICGtesting.com
Printed in the USA
FSOW02n1537280915
11629FS